Be ENCOURAGED

As You Follow Your Dreams & Visions

Be Encouraged,

Live Encouraged,

Stay Encouraged,

Published by
ENCOURAGING LIFE ENTERPRISES

Written by **EDNA WAYNE MATHEWS**

BE ENCOURAGED
As You Follow Your Dreams & Visions

Copyright © 2017 by Edna Wayne Mathews

All rights reserved. No portion of this publication may be reproduced, transmitted in any form or by any means, electronic, mechanical, photocopy, recording, or otherwise, without the prior permission of the author. Brief quotations may be used in literary reviews or special occasions.

Scripture quotations have been listed at the end of the book

First Edition

Published by
ENCOURAGING LIFE ENTERPRISES

www.EdnaWayneMathews.com

EncouragingLife@yahoo.com

Facebook, Twitter, Instagram, Pinterest, LinkedIn

ISBN: 978-0-692-79530-9

LCCN#: Library of Congress Control Number: 2016917374

Category: Self-Help / Motivational & Inspirational / Faith

Foreword by Dr. Michelle Johnson, Joyce Feaster, Willie Rivers, Melba Redmond and Jennifer Ward

Edited by Miriam Mèndez

Developmentally Edited by Willie Rivers

Cover Designed by Eli-The Book Guy

Formatted by Eli Sir. and Jahshua E. Blyden | CrunchTime Graphics

Dedications

This book is a love letter to my darling son, daughter, grandson and granddaughters, nieces, great niece, and spiritual-daughters, and to every person in pursuit of big dreams and visions. I am sharing my pioneering entrepreneurial journey so that you may **"Be Encouraged"** as you move forward with confidence into your amazing God given destiny.

BE ENCOURAGED – *As You Follow Your Dreams & Visions*

Acknowledgements

My spiritual journey is a process directed by God. Without a doubt my first and highest praise, thanksgiving, and honor is to my Lord and Savior, Jesus Christ. Just as in Jeremiah, I am assured that before I was in my mother's womb He called me by name, and He gave me purpose (1:5). Thank you my Lord. I will always seek to glorify You, through the gifts you have given me.

To my belated parents, my family, and everyone who have propelled my faith's growth; thank you.

Thank you to Willie Rivers, my editor and lifelong friend. While I completed this book, he continued to inspire and provide: true, steadfast, enduring support, advice, assurance, and hope.

– Edna Wayne Mathews

BE ENCOURAGED – *As You Follow Your Dreams & Visions*

My Goal

"For my hope is that their hearts may be encouraged as they are knit together in [unselfish] love, ... so that they may have all the riches that come from the full assurance of understanding the joy of salvation, resulting in a true [and more intimate] knowledge of the mystery of God, that is, Christ" (Colossians 2:2 Amp).

* * *

Be Encouraged

The raising of one's confidence and hope.

* * *

BE ENCOURAGED – *As You Follow Your Dreams & Visions*

Contents

Dedications iii
Acknowledgements v
My Goal vii
Be Encouraged vii
Foreword xi

Chapter 1
Uniquely Called "Recognizing Your Purpose" 1
   Uniquely Qualified *5*

Chapter 2
Yea Though I Walked Through The Valley and Shadows......... 7
   An Inauspicious Beginning *7*
   The Foundation of My Faith *9*
   Trial or Inconvenience *10*

Chapter 3
All Things Are Possible To Him Who Believes 13
   Discovering My Divine Destiny *14*
   Discovering Who I am; Whose I am; and Whose I am not! .. *15*
   Proper Care for His Temple *16*
   Accepting God's Vision for My Life *19*
   Dreams and Visions Meet Opportunity *21*

Chapter 4

God Turns Opportunity into Reality 25
   The Importance of Your Spiritual Coach *26*
   David vs. Goliath...Overcoming the Foe *27*
   Strong and Courageous in the Lord *32*
   My Defining Moment *34*

Chapter 5

A Need for Encouragement 37
   Becoming an Encourager *39*

Chapter 6

Becoming Spirit-Builders 43

Chapter 7

Six Godly Principles for Success in Business and Life 45
   I. PUT GOD FIRST *45*
   II. WRITE YOUR VISION DOWN *48*
   III. DREAM BIG *54*
   IV. GO FOR THE GOAL *59*
   V. GO THROUGH THE VALLEY *62*
   VI. BE AN ENCOURAGER! *71*

Daily Prayers & Confessions 81
My Prayer for You 82
Self-Reflections 83
About The Author 107

Foreword

"I could not put the book down. I was blessed by the six principles. I'm putting those into practice. I was blessed reading it".
— Dr. Michelle Johnson, Assistant Professor, Physical Medicine and Rehabilitation; Director of the Rehabilitation Robotics Lab

* * *

"Readers, you are in for a divine blessing! Many years ago, Edna mentioned that there was a book that God was telling her to write, and I am excited that she has finally accomplished that, which she has been lead to do, publishing her book, **"BE ENCOURAGED…** *As You Follow Your Dreams & Visions"*. As she has been inspired to share this work with us and to help us to have the courage to pursue our dreams; let us apply these powerful nuggets of wisdom that she offers to fulfill God's plans for our lives.

Edna is a truly gifted, intelligent, compassionate entrepreneur, and woman of God: An anointed teacher and ministry leader in our church. Edna has shared the foundation of faith with many throughout the years. She not only shares her revelation knowledge with others, as she does in **"BE ENCOURAGED…** *As You Follow Your Dreams & Visions"*, but is always available to pray a prayer of faith with you, through whatever situation you may be facing. It is clear that she continues to spend much time alone with 'my' Father, and we benefit from the fruit of her study time".

— Joyce Feaster, HR Corporate Officer

* * *

"After editing and then closely reading the book, I can attest that **"BE ENCOURAGED...*As You Follow Your Dreams & Visions"***, is not a "vanity project". It is a well written journal of Ms. Mathews' journey from a rural Louisiana childhood to successful careers; as a teacher, social worker, high-fashion model, and finally, the realization of her dream as an entrepreneur. Weaving a wonderful thread through her faith-led life journey are well used scriptural references that she used to guide her to achieving her entrepreneurship dream. I am certain that they will inspire and also guide you.

Read the book and feel the love and encouragement flow through it. Keep it by your bedside - and maybe, just maybe- it will help you to **"BE ENCOURAGED...*As You Follow Your Dreams & Visions"***.

– Willie Rivers, Retired Corporate Executive

* * *

"**Edna is a spiritual mentor!** Her light of love is so very bright and inviting. In this book, Edna shares her life journey with the reader, and simultaneously builds their confidence based on the word of God. Quickly, one can become complacent and reluctant, to walk in their divine destiny as a result of fear, lack of knowledge, and negativity. In this book, Edna discusses how she overcame numerous obstacles in her life; as a result of her faith, encouragement, and affirmations from the Word of God.

As I read the book, I felt an awakening in my spirit. It helped me to identity what gifts lie dormant that I could resurrect, how I can help others, and walk out the will of God for my life. **"BE ENCOURAGED...*As You Follow Your Dreams & Visions"***, will tug at your heart, inspire you to dream big, and motivate you to capture your vision and bring it to life".

– Melba Redmond, RN, MSN Nurse Educator

* * *

"Edna Mathews is an example of God's grace in motion. Her spirit shines through her bright hazel eyes, and just by being in her presence. She is an inspiration to me, as one of her many spiritual daughters.

"BE ENCOURAGED...*As You Follow Your Dreams & Visions"*, gives us a glimpse into Edna's life, by showing us how God's grace has always been with her. When I read the book, Edna's stories show me that God is with all of us. **"BE ENCOURAGED...*As You Follow Your Dreams & Visions"***, gives you the strength to pursue your dreams, even when life throws you unexpected curve balls".

– Jennifer Ward, Grants and Contracts Analyst

Be Encouraged

As You Follow Your Dreams & Visions

Be Encouraged,

Live Encouraged

Stay Encouraged

BE ENCOURAGED – *As You Follow Your Dreams & Visions*

CHAPTER 1

Uniquely Called
"Recognizing Your Purpose"

* * *

Have you been called or commissioned to be a world-changer? Like the Israelites, have you been wandering around in your desert of life for what seems like your own forty years? Have you strayed from the path of your passion, that dream you have always had? Or, are you still trying to figure out, "what is my purpose in life?" Recognizing your purpose, and how to fulfill it, can sometimes be challenging. However, these challenges can be overcome, through a solid foundation in Jesus Christ, and by acquiring a strong, encouraging support base.

All of God's children are given this special spiritual gift. This gift is named, "the fruit of the spirit". Just think, it took one fruit of the Holy Spirit to yield in us nine unlimited attributes, which are; **"love, joy, peace, long-suffering, gentleness, goodness, faith, meekness, and temperance"** (Galatians 5:22-23). This boundless spiritual gift, produces a visible change in us, that exemplifies our Lord and savior, Jesus Christ. This foundation brings about unconditional victories through Him. The fruit of the spirit forms in us a lifestyle, where we can show pure love, one for another, by willingly being helpful to each other. John 13:34 reveals, God's big vision is that we are *"to love one another"*, in the same manner that we are called to love Him.

I already knew, that in order to achieve our God given dreams, we must be changed into the love of the Lord. His unique plan for fulfilling our God given dreams and vision is directly woven together into our willingness to inspire, encourage, and to be helpful to one another. *"Give and it shall be given unto you, good measures pressed down, shaken together, running over, shall men give into your bosom"* (Luke 6:38). When we bless each other through our support and encouragement to one another, we will receive the rewards of our amazing gifts. Philippians 4:19 assures, *"God will supply all of our needs."*

He will keep us on our path, and take care of our needs. It is His will that we should desire to bless someone else, just as God desires to bless us. In our doing so, He can and will bless us. King Solomon, the wisest man to ever live, said, *"I know that there is nothing better for people than to be happy and to do good while they live"* (Ecclesiastes 3:12). We are uniquely called to demonstrate His manner of love to the world. Our uniquely called purpose is to be a reflection of His goodness in everything we do; then, we can live much more meaningful lives. He will bless and provide for the dreams and visions He has created in us.

"Be Encouraged!" The big dreams God gives us may be overwhelming. They are bigger than what we can imagine. But, do not be fearful or in doubt. However, be aware of the self-destructive seeds of fear and doubt. They *will* produce the contaminating fruit of procrastination, insecurity, pride, low-self-esteem, despair, embarrassment, depression, worry, and shame. These are just some of the lethal weapons that can create the defeating feeling of self-doubt. The scripture John 10:10 explains, their purpose is *"to steal, kill, and destroy"*. Then, why be encouraged, you may ask? Because God has placed greatness in you! *"You are a holy people to the LORD your God..."* (Deuteronomy 7:6). It is true, on our own, we will get lost in the dark-wilderness of defeat. The truth is, every one of us, at one time or another, have gotten off track in our lives. We have all been at the bottom, of a seemingly endless pit of despair, fear, or anger. Oh, but, His word is our GPS network (God's Positioning System), to guide us to where we belong. It is our God's Positioning System that restores, heals, delivers, renews, and inspires us to **"Be Encouraged"**. *"God has given each of you a gift from His great variety of spiritual gifts. Use them well to serve one another"* (I Peter 4:10). Jesus explained why God sent Him as our gift into the world. He came, *"that we may have life and life more abundantly"* (John 10:10). It is God's plan that we should have an abundant destiny. Our abundant destiny is based on His principle of serving one another, through love. And, only through His love, can we righteously do great and mighty things. If you are an entrepreneur, businessperson, educator, student, parent, or whom ever you are; **"Be Encouraged"**. He has instructed us to, *"Arm yourselves likewise with the same mind"* (Luke 4:1). To truly operate in the dreams and visions God has given for our lives, we must be willing to give to others with unrestricted love. Then, trust that God, and God alone, will supply our needs, even when we cannot see it. I had learned that He will make available the resources to meet our needs.

Running my small business and pursuing my God given dream was a spiritual journey, as much as, a road trip to my success. In this highly charged, roller-coaster economy, the people of God must remember: If you honor God with your faith and obedience, He *will "direct your path"* (Proverbs 3:6). When God calls you, know that you can do it! Yes, you can!!!

There came a time, when I heard Him call me to be one of His temple-keepers; right in the middle of pursuing my own business goals. His call was transforming. This is a transformation that only God can provide through our surrendering to Him. I had learned the key to being a success! God has called all of His children to honor and care for His temple; to be "temple-keepers". Even in my business, this is what I was called to do. The word teaches us that this gifted calling is God's will, because Isaiah 49:1 affirms, ***"Before I was born, the Lord called me to serve Him."*** Being a "temple-keeper", required my commitment to spiritual and physical discipline. What we see, hear, and speak define our spiritual discipline. Our physical discipline manifests itself in our diet, exercise, rest, and other lifestyle activities. It entails being a steward to the unique calling He has placed in me.

My purpose was to share His word through my lifestyle and my works; by helping lift and raise the confidence, faith, and hope of others. I had learned, in business life as in everyday life, His unique calling is for us to do that which God has already established and planned for our lives. Isaiah 30:21 tells us, ***"Whether you turn to the right or to the left, your ears will hear a voice behind you, saying, 'This is the way; walk in it'."*** When we follow the path God has designed for His children's lives, we then help to bring order to the plan He has for the world. This very same unique calling is in each of our lives. Yes, you too are uniquely called. He had confirmed to me His call to love Him and to love one another, with all our heart, soul, and strength, meant that every area of our spiritual and physical lives must be seen as belonging to Christ, through His kingdom's purpose.

Uniquely Qualified

Like the Israelite's along the road, there will come a time, when you too, will be tested through being pressed, stretched, and stressed in every way; in your spirit, business, and everyday life.

The nuggets of wisdom in this book, from my life's journey, are designed to give you the much needed **"Be Encouraged"** guidance to inspire and empower you to pursue your dreams, because God has uniquely qualified you.

BE ENCOURAGED – *As You Follow Your Dreams & Visions*

CHAPTER 2

Yea Though I Walked Through The Valley and Shadows...

Psalms (23:4)

* * *

An Inauspicious Beginning

Entrepreneurship has long been in my blood! It first was revealed in the form of dreams. Dreams filled with unimaginable details and intriguing crystal clear images. They were so much bigger than I could fully comprehend at my young age. Can you too relate to having such a dream? Has God also given you such crystal clear dreams? Dreams just for you? Dreams to prosper you? Dreams to take you from where you are, to expand your possibilities (I Chronicles 4:10)?

The fact is, everyone has dreams. The reality is, all dreams are not God inspired. Dreams with visions from God are beautiful, vibrant, and supernatural. Filled with exciting possibilities, hopes, and plans; they are a vision of what He has planned just for you. Visions with details so brilliant you can hardly contain them all by yourself. They are dreams that resonate something very special in you. Oh, how exciting!

However, from the very beginning of my life, I could have been counted out and never allowed to achieve any of my dreams. I was born the fifth of six children, in the rural Louisiana Delta. I was told by my mother that on the frigid, early February morning, when I was born, it was the absolute coldest and iciest day she had ever seen. What I know personally is that it would be the first of many challenges, and I could have not made it without God.

Born a tiny, premature baby, I suffered and fought with a number of health issues shortly after birth. By the age of three years, with a weak respiratory system, I was stricken with severe pneumonia, suffered with bronchitis, and whooping cough on three different occasions. As a very small and struggling baby, God gave me the enduring weapon of tenacity to fight and to establish my place in His destiny plan.

Very early, I learned that God will use whatever trials that come, as special preparation, to launch you into His plans for your future. Even as a fledgling toddler, well before I was able to understand the meaning of faith, I believed. In my young understanding, I knew there was *something* already deep inside of me, which allowed me to believe; "I am here for a purpose". Lord, **"You will give me hidden treasures, riches stored in secret places, so that I may know that You are the Lord ... who summons me by name"** (Isaiah 45:3).

God's love for us is before our beginning and it is for evermore. In the book of Jeremiah, He affirmed His love and plans for us. Before Jeremiah (1:5) was conceived in his mother's womb, God knew him, in the same manner, which he knows us. When birthed into this world, God had already placed purpose in him. Just as He has for you and me.

Early on, the doctors diagnosed that I was suffering from a very painful and crippling congenital disorder in my left leg; which was yet to be defined or understood. To try to help straighten, strengthen, and lengthen my leg; I wore, big, awkward, and heavy clunky iron braces, 'day and night'. By school age, my medical files were almost as tall as I was. Still, I could hardly walk. The big cumbersome braces nearly weighed more than my little body. The pain and heavy weight were so tremendously crippling. Through this very beginning I learned about trusting God.

The Foundation of My Faith

As a child, I was drawn to my mother's singing and praises, all throughout the day. She sang and praised, all the time. His Spirit would fill the house. It was just as sweet as the fresh aroma, from the beautiful velvety pink flowers on the lilac tree, just outside our front windows, on a bright spring morning. When I asked her, "why she sang so much?" She would say, "Oh, baby, I am spending time with God." My little heart felt His surpassing peace. It set an atmosphere in our home, as well as, in my heart. I was learning that it was our special time with God.

Day after day, I heard my mother's continual request, "Please Father, heal my baby's leg." Her song and prayer was filled with such joyous praise, almost as if He was there. Surely, she was there in the presence of God's glory. I sensed there was an intimate conversation, a personal request, that she completely surrendered to God. Sometimes, as I listened, I would slowly crawl on the floor into a corner and rest there; in the atmosphere of her praise. It gave me a peaceful assurance.

The doctor visits were unrelenting. In due course, between my doctors and my parents, the decision was made that I would start school the following year, at the age of seven. All through my school years I became very familiar with pain. Ultimately, the doctors concluded that my left leg would be permanently disabled and shorter than my right one.

I soon learned the divine principle of, **"Call that which is not as though it already is"** (Romans 4:17). As far back as I could remember, everything within me always believed that I would walk *naturally*. While my mother was praising God, her faith flowed into me. I "claimed" my leg's healing. Additionally, I absolutely refused to accept this disorder, especially the doctor's reports. With every ounce of my being, I would force myself to walk as upright as possible; and regularly, I participated in typical childhood activities. The issues with my leg became the fertile ground for my faith. I could not see it, at the time, but I believed it was going to happen, and I was going to walk naturally.

Trial or Inconvenience

Growing up, I was determined to never allow pain or my present circumstances to define me…, and "that" was the only option. It was a challenging effort, but daily my mother and I worked hard to help me overcome my diagnosis. The next school year, I was able to attend without the usage of the big heavy and embarrassing iron braces. Still I had to wear them after school and during the night. My little, long, and slender body jetted into a growth spurt, and I grew taller and taller. As I became older, I was more and more determined to walk unencumbered. Consequently, very few people really knew the true extent of my medical problems.

Just at the point of learning to deal with the crippling leg pain, another medical issue arose. In junior high school, puberty had already begun to mature my body. I started to experience another type of unbearable, incapacitating, and very debilitating pain. Every month I suffered severe abdominal cramps. My doctor diagnosed it to be, "just extremely bad menstrual cramps". My cramps and menstrual flow would last abnormally long periods of times. It was not unusual for it to last up to ten, twelve, or even fourteen days. I was also chronically anemic.

Along with my leg pains, as I grew older, the cramps continued to worsen. Nevertheless, I fully enjoyed participating in my high school experience. I was active in my school choir, drama club, student government, and other school events. I excelled academically and graduated in the top ten percent of my class; and reigned as class debutante in high school. Never doubting my acceptance to the college of my choice; I was rewarded a college scholarship.

By my freshmen year in college, the two pains seemed to have "joined-forces". Once again, I was hardly able to walk. Through means of medical advancements, the doctors performed a knee replacement surgery, and over time, the pain improved. I was able to get back on track. During this season, I was a debutante and also dating a young man; who soon after proposed. During my senior year we were married. However, the sharp, cruel, death-gripping, and hostile cramps grew even more persistent.

The pain was more and more severe. The menstrual pain was no longer monthly, but daily. The excruciating and agonizing pain had grown completely unbearable; I was extremely ill. Month after month the heavy, unpredictable, and flooding menstrual cycle worsened. Only one semester from graduation, with the ratchet, weakening pain consuming my body, I was still determined to finish college. It finally got to the point where it took me an entire class period to get from my car to class; I was just too weak. The cramps completely interrupted my life, and I had no strength left. My body was utterly shutting down.

During Christmas semester break, the illness suddenly became more critical. I was rushed to the hospital; immediately, a major emergency, eight-hour surgery was performed. After years of being misdiagnosed, this long, dreadful, and evasive pain was finally correctly diagnosed; as severe Endometriosis. To add insult to injury, I learned I had been misdiagnosed only because of my race.

Feeling the lack of value, I felt a conflicting emotional range of emotions; from joy and happiness, to unavoidable anger, and finally a deep sense of betrayal. I had suffered this severe, excruciating, and painful disorder since puberty; simply because, at that time, it was a condition typically only looked for in *white* women. For that simplistic reason, this illness was not properly diagnosed in me. In spite of this moment, I was still so thankful to know God.

While moving through my early life's journey, *I was learning the lesson and deep understanding of true faith,* as defined in Hebrews 11:1, **"Now faith is confidence in what we hope for, and assurance about what we do not see."** I was trusting in God, for what I was hoping for, and believing in His assured expectancy.

CHAPTER 3

All Things Are Possible To Him Who Believes

Matthew 9:22

* * *

My early challenges were not just long and numerous, but also lonely and very painful. To the natural mind, it might have appeared that my conditions were too constraining, and it might have determined my course of life. The fact is the Lord restored my leg, and healed my body from severe pain.

I completed college with a B.A. degree in Sociology and Social Work, moved to Wisconsin with my new husband, and started my career in Social Work. During that time, by God's grace, I became a successful high-fashion model in the most demanding and competitive beauty-fashion market in the world, New York City!!! I traveled along stunning highways with beautiful vistas and landscapes. My life was much bigger than I could have ever dreamed. There, I discovered a new "road less traveled", my passion for the skincare industry. I loved it!

Discovering My Divine Destiny

In the glamour world, the mirage of beauty; looking good, maintaining flawless skin, perfect figures, and impeccable health and wellness was all around, all to give the appearance of perfection. Yet, I was fully aware, who better than I to know, that "Life is not perfect. Life is what you can believe and make it to be". Jesus said *(to me),* ***"If you can believe, all things are possible to him who believes"*** (Mark 9:23). I had learned that how I saw myself was the bridge that connects me to my abilities.

After several years, my rigorously intense high fashion modeling schedule, became too brutally demanding on my knee. I had modeled for some of the leading fashion designers, and the industry continued to inspire me. However, in my spirit, I could feel the Lord shifting my focus. It was time for me, to pursue my passionate desire to open my business and become an entrepreneur. My success in modeling was a road trip, right to the front door of my inspired destiny.

As I began to pursue the business God had shown me, He began to cause me to examine my faith with a fine-tooth comb. He had challenged me with this profound life changing question, ***"Do you not know that your body is the temple of the Holy Spirit, who is in you, whom you have received from God? You are not your own; you were bought at a price. Therefore, honor God with your body"*** (I Corinthians 6:19).

I experienced a compelling revelation from God. I was swept off my feet. As never before, my eyes were opened with the light of truth. I realized that when my spirit is free of the "mirage", I am then able to use my inherited gift from God; to willingly breathe life of encouragement into others. II Timothy 4:5 encourages, ***"You should keep a clear mind in every situation... Work at telling others***

the Good News, and fully carry out the ministry God has given you. " He affirmed, ***"My goal is that they may Be Encouraged... I want them to have complete confidence that they understand God's mysterious plan..."*** (Colossians 2:2). God continued to draw me in His direction. In my spirit, I knew that God's plan and ministry for me, in both my spiritual and business life, was to build-up and inspire others to accept and appreciate the "highest self" that He has given.

The word of God established it. When our spirit is free of false clutter, we are then able to do the great and mighty things God has appointed us to do. We are all called to inspire each other, to **"Be Encouraged"** by willingly raising confidence, and hope in each other.

Discovering Who I am; Whose I am; and Whose I am not!

In pursuing our dreams and visions, it is easy to become discouraged. Some among us are discouraged because of how we perceive ourselves, others through accomplishments, titles, college degrees, or the work we do. Others may feel a sense of discouragement, based on guilt and shame from past failures, family legacy, low self-esteem, personal appearance, and misplaced value judgments. Through this, I came to understand that many of us were judging ourselves and others through prisms of contradictions; engaging in the false clutter of betrayals, hurts, rejections, conceits, and deceits; all the while, constantly striving for approval, acceptance, and encouragements for ourselves.

God showed me that these contradictions were lies authored by brokenness. The Holy Spirit was taking me up to a higher place of understanding; my life was transforming. Not only did He boldly clarify *who I am; whose I am; whose I am NOT,* and *how and why I came to exist;* but also, *what I am to do.* I realized that the truth of our identity is founded on how God sees us. Rooted in these truths, God taught me the encouraging compassion available through Him. What "good news"!

Through the storms in my life, I gained infallible foundational treasures. Through Him I learned to encourage myself, to become my self-advocate, and to be strong. I definitely learned the powerful impact of taking action. There are those certain things about "self" which I could and can change. James 2:14-26 taught me that faith without works is dead. God's challenge was a complete spiritual awakening. Our body is not our own. He gave us this body and declared it the temple; where the Holy Spirit of God dwells. Therefore, our bodies are more important than the well-kept pristine monuments, synagogues, church buildings, or finest houses. It is the Holy Spirit's residence, which is on lease to us from God (I Corinthians 1:27). Oh, how humbling!

Proper Care for His Temple

As His word soaked in deeper, my spirit was immersed and saturated by His charge. I pondered the question, "Does the world really understand the divinely supernatural connection (oneness) between our body and the Holy Spirit?" Does the world realize, "That we are given the privilege to use His temple, and to serve as caretakers of the home of the Holy Spirit?" Does the world truly comprehend the royal priesthood of our body? "Does it realize that our body is the physical temple for the "Most-High Spirit"; to live in, to guide, and shepherd our lives?" My light bulb came on. My answer is, yes!

"When God saw His work, (He said) all was very good." (Genesis 1:31). God affirmed Himself and His handy work. He formed this temple, our bodies, as the works of His perfect hands. *"We are his workmanship, created <u>in</u> Christ Jesus..."* (Ephesians 2:10).

In my transformation, I was captivated by the compelling, revealing conviction; between the single-minded indwelling Holy Spirit and the seamless requirement of keeping His temple 'looking good and feeling good,' both spiritually and physically. I had been pierced by the challenge from God Himself (I Corinthians 6:29). On a much higher level, I understood His important command. I was to help dispel the prevailing contradiction, of having to choose one verses the other, when both are essential for an honest relationship with God.

We are to beautify, groom, wash, purge, and refresh His spiritual and physical temple daily. God had shown me, that our body and spirit are one. Our bodies are the sanctuary for the Holy Spirit of God, to live (be active) in this world. He revealed to me that we cannot continue to neglect, debase, and destroy the foundation of the temple of God; while at the same time proclaiming the presence of His spirit. *"Their loyalty is divided between God and the world, and they are unstable in everything they do"* (James 1:8). *"If anyone destroys God's temple, God will destroy that person; for God's temple is sacred, and you together are that temple"* (I Corinthians 3:17).

Our physical health, wellness, and outer grooming is a symbolic reflection of our inner spirit. *"Anyone who listens to the word, but does not do what it says is like someone who looks at his face in a mirror, and, after looking at himself, goes away and <u>immediately</u>*

forgets what he looks like" (James 1:23). A temple-keeper, *"Is a lamp to the world"* (Matthew 5:14).

He confirmed my vision and anchored my faith. He uncluttered my ability to hear Him and to receive Him. God affirmed His will for me, to inspire and encourage others to walk in His purpose. His voice is calling out to His temple keepers, **"You are the light of the world"** (Matthew 5:15). I now knew this was my mission, my position in life; to help bring light into the world; through living the truth of God's love for both our spiritual and physical bodies.

As His temple-keepers, our Father will use every righteously developed nugget which He has placed in our treasure chest; to help remove spiritual misunderstandings which shackle the people (temples) of God. The enemies of this world have distorted and hold captive His most precious creation; by perverting the minds and hearts of His temple-keepers.

We, the temple-keepers, have been reckless with His temple care. Specifically, by misusing, abusing, neglecting, and setting limits on the importance of the physical well-being of the spiritual residence; His Holy temple. *"My people are destroyed for lack of knowledge; because you have rejected knowledge"* (Hosea 4:6). When we take proper care of God's Holy temple, we become aligned with His purpose and plan for us. *"You see, at just the right time, when we were still powerless, Christ died for the ungodly"* (Roman 5:6). Our body is a gift from heaven, created in the image of God, to value God. He wants us to honor Him not only with our spirit, but also our bodies.

Today, our computerized communication networks are regularly contaminated with viral infection, which corrupt and weaken our operating systems. He had shown me, that in the same manner, our temple care system has been corrupted. We have become separated from God's true plan; from His empirical standard of loving and caring for each other, as we love our own body. We are to care for His temple. Over and over He aligned our love for each other, by reminding us of the love He has for us; *"**A new command I give you: Love one another. As I have loved you, so you must love** one **another**"* (Matthew 22:39; John 13:34). *"**Carry each other's burdens, and in this way you will fulfill the law of Christ**"* (Galatians 6:2).

Spirit clutter has entered in and consumed the hearts, clouded our spiritual and physical selves. His covenant-caretaker relationship requires us to use our platforms that He has given us, to restore and breathe life back into His temples. He tells us that, when our mind, body, and soul is available to God, we *"**Put on the new self, created to be like God in true righteousness and holiness**"* (Ephesians 4:24). God has challenged His children, to be both physical and spiritual temple-keepers. Has He been tugging at your heart too; to use your platform to reach out to others and to help bring His light to the world?

Accepting God's Vision for My Life

I saw with clarity God's vision for temple care. Then, with deep humility, I realized the nuggets in my life which He had built-up, strengthened, and refined in me over the years, would be used to glorify Him. He also allowed me to take a stroll along the glamour avenues of life. In that moment, I knew without a doubt, that my spectacular seasons and plans for modeling would be turned around and used for His purpose. His plans were greater than my plans, and only He could get the glory. I learned that He will allow us certain experiences in our lives. So, that at the right time, He will use them to become generous blessings to others and to glorify Him.

Keeping my physical body and skin well-groomed was a natural requirement for a modeling career. Regularly, I indulged in the benefits of rejuvenating therapeutic spa services. While doing so, I became more and more fascinated by the skin, body care, and wellness industry. Every time there was an opportunity, I probed deeper into this *transformative*, and self-esteem boosting personal care, and wellness industry. Most intriguing to me, was the bold and newly emerging field of Aesthetic; recent to the U.S. marketplace. Now, driven by a greater purpose and overflowing with excitement, I researched and gathered information regarding the exploding professional European skincare industry. It was right on the cutting edge; and so was I.

God had previously shown me that every journey in our lives is sprinkled with nuggets of treasured jewels, that lead us to His plan. Even then, tucked away under the umbrella of my pioneer undertaking, the Lord was equipping me to use my nuggets of treasured jewels; which I had gained along the way, for a new opportunity.

Amazingly, one day, the door of opportunity opened to me; an invitation to study at Europe's foremost and finest, skin and wellness institute. I recognized that a blessing had come my way, and immediately I shifted into gear. There was so much to learn! Every aspect of study required keen, professional people skills, along with refined and proficient clinician knowledge.

Aesthetic was my passion. I loved it!!! While studying and practicing the intricacies of the professional skin, body care, and wellness industry; I soaked it all up, acquired new knowledge, and volunteered for everything. Upon successfully completing the institute's world renowned program, I was speechless and filled with humility, when I was acknowledged as "the most outstanding student Aesthetician". Needless to say, I was the first and only African American to receive certification.

Dreams and Visions Meet Opportunity

While still in my tender twenties, I launched into another journey of faith. Staying focused on my vision and equipped with God's grace, guidance, and my determination; I started my first business. I was elated! I had "done it"!!! In this emerging, futurist business market, I became the first African American Aesthetician in the United States of America. God had blessed my talents as an Aesthetician and my abilities in business. I was overjoyed! I had become a pioneer, an entrepreneur, a businesswoman, and founder of Edel's Day Spa. I was on my way to my God given destiny. From the ground up, I built the first full service day spa in the State of Wisconsin, and one of only a few throughout the country. It was ground breaking.

You never know *who is watching you*, but you can rest assured someone is. Therefore, ***"Whatsoever ye do in word or deed, do all in the name of the Lord Jesus"*** (Colossians 3:17). Shortly after opening my first location, I was approached by a business agent from a major international, corporate commercial development group. They petitioned me, for Edel's Day Spa, to become a member tenant in their newly planned upscale, commercial retail development center. This was a major worldwide corporate development group, and the most intimidating step of my life. I felt a whole *popcorn bag* of emotions; so excited and thrilled, yet, overwhelmed, nervous, insecure, frightened, inadequate, and inferior; just to mention a few.

Although I was very familiar with contracts, I was fearful of this type of contract negotiation, at such a high corporate business level.

On the other hand, in spite of all my vast emotional uncertainties, I was oh, so, so thankful and overcome with excitement! God was about to promote the gifts and talents He had given me; to a much, much larger market. To a stage bigger than I could ever have imagined.

Once again, God kept telling me to **"Be Encouraged"**. My dreams and visions had come face-to-face with opportunity. However, my greatest and most overwhelming anxiety was the finances. While there were business plans, designs, construction, contracts, negotiations, project planning, suppliers, inventory, staff, hiring, and on-and-on, my biggest concern was securing the finances. I did not have the advantage of "old family money" or personal wealth.

However, by this time, I had learned how to and from whom to seek direction. Matthew 6:33 tells us just what to do; ***"Seek first the kingdom of God and His righteousness, then, all these things taken together will be given unto you (me)."***

I sought the Lord; to get alone, in His presence. In my quiet place the Lord stilled my spirit. Everything within me knew this was God. There, He reminded me how important it was to reach back, into the treasure chest of my life; to seek the resources that He had stored up for my future. He reminded me of the faith, trust, dependence, perseverance, endurance, strength, and wisdom; also of the dreams and visions He had placed in me. He assured me that I had the *treasure sources* to handle much bigger life challenges. He reminded me:

- It was He who gave me life into this world, and while I was sick as a premature infant, he protected me.
- He had stretched, strengthened my leg, and made me to walk; "Correctly".

- When I was so ill that I could have died, He put me in the hands of just the right medical care; always at just the right time.

- He removed the attacks against my health, and made me whole and complete. It was He who healed my body.

- When I was told I would never walk properly He proved His promises. Furthermore, I became a successful high fashion model.

- He gifted and trusted me as the first African American Aesthetician.

- He opened every door that was closed. And finally, how He, yes He, prepared me to enter this door.

I started setting quality time aside for the presence of the Lord God Almighty. Making myself available to listen and reflect. Therefore, allowing myself to be saturated with the truth. Then, I fell on my knees and gave Him all praise and thanksgiving. There I surrendered my fearful anxieties into the Lord's hands. One "lump" at a time He removed them. Like dust in a rug, God shook-off the fear in me, and once again I was plugged back into my power-source. I recharged and "stirred-up" His *spiritual nuggets* within me: my faith, trust, endurance, perseverance, determination, patience, joy, peace, and my courage. The fruitfulness of His spirit, were all there. He had renewed my vision and given me direction.

BE ENCOURAGED – *As You Follow Your Dreams & Visions*

CHAPTER 4

God Turns Opportunity into Reality

* * *

I began consulting with my business lawyer and banker to start the process of planning for my new business. Although my work was cut out for me I was armed, inspired, and ready.

Perhaps, you too are like me. God truly gives us *inspired* dreams and visions. What are yours? He literally gave me *dreams and purpose* for my business. I could see in my mind clear details, images, and thoughts; road maps to my marvelous goals. The more I meditated, fervently communed with God about my dreams, the purpose became crystal clear. They were continuously in my mind; day and night.

To ensure I completely captured the visions and dreams God had for me, I slept with pen and a "vision notebook" on my night stand. I carried them with me *where ever* I went. My wealth of *spiritual nuggets*, stored up as personal possessions in my life's treasure chest, were also my constant companion. I was filled with the same nervousness that I had experienced, so many times before, while modeling. At the same time, I was bursting with excitement. *"I did not regard myself as having laid hold of it yet; but one thing I do: forgetting what lies behind and reaching forward to what lies ahead"* (Philippians 3:13). I set out to learn the process required for me to acquire approval of a Small Business Administration (SBA) Loan.

Straightaway, it was as if I had run into a tall, thick steel armored wall; confronted with racism, sexism, and ageism. What I immediately learned was that African Americans were not historically awarded business loans, neither conventional nor SBA. Moreover, I could not have begun to imagine the impossible odds for an African American woman; and more so, the numerous challenges for a very young African American woman.

I quickly realized the pathway to change is very slow. But, I had already been prepared by God. I learned that *when God makes a promise, it MUST come to pass*, if you just stick-to-it. This journey to bring together the plans and finances which God supplied for my business, took well over three years. As a young African American woman, in my twenties, I launched into another incredible journey of faith. Again, much bigger than me and greater than I had ever imagined.

The Importance of Your Spiritual Coach

May I encourage you to seek out and listen to your spiritual coach? Who is your spiritual coach you ask? Your spiritual coach is the Holy Spirit, your guide; *"God is Spirit"* (John 4:24). It is that comforting, up-lifting voice from with-in. At the moment you connect with your guiding Spirit, He will lead you to a heightened level of peace, joy, and perfect clarity; resulting in overwhelming excitement. With His Spirit the Lord encouraged me to have faith in my strengths. He planted His seed in me. I knew He would multiply it (II Cor. 9:10). By then, I had already come to understand that His multiplication always produces blessings.

Over the years the seed of faith had developed in me a series of skills, knowledge, and experiences. I applied my college education, experience in Sociology and Social Work, my skin and wellness skills, along with the essential business knowledge I acquired through modeling; combined them with my treasure chest of *spiritual nuggets*, and set out on my journey to achieve my dreams. In other words, I packaged my *less-than-enough and His more-than-enough,* together with my awareness of who *I know* God to be!

David vs. Goliath…Overcoming the Foe

However, the road to becoming the first African American woman to secure a major small business loan, was extremely rugged and grueling. It was indeed, more difficult than one could have ever imagined. My achievement came during an era when the SBA and conventional financing process was not, in any way, *"user-friendly"* to minorities and women. There were no federal mandates to ensure access to capital for minorities and women. Furthermore, the institutions of the grand-wizards of racism and discrimination were indeed factors. But, God promised, ***"All things work together for the good of those that are called by His name according to His purpose"*** (Romans 8:28).

I came to realize that the long, painful stretching treatment process to heal my leg had also helped prepare me, once again, for the long, painful journey of this walk. In an amazing, "around-about-sort-of-away," those long agonizing bouts with my health, as well as being a young African American woman, all proved to be empowering resources. Those experiences, together with growing up in the deep-southern Delta, shadowed by the acute presence of overt racism, sustained me in my resolve to achieve my dreams. Because of my young age and naiveté, I had no idea of the countless, disheartening, silent, and often invisible types of institutional barricades that existed. Neither did I know that the many U-turns, road blocks, and hoops within that system were all designed for me to jump through.

The challenges or simply put, barriers, soon became clear. They were hidden traps set to defeat, or at a minimum to discourage me. The challenges were more difficult than I could have ever imagined. However, my commitment to secure financing was truly so *much bigger than me*.

Growing up in the Deep South, I had experienced the penetrating and wretched effects of racism; both personal and institutional. The racism that I faced as a youth was very overt, designed to mentally, psychologically, emotionally, and economically *cripple African Americans*; serving to maintain the social order of "separate and unequal". Racism has a complex and cumulative effect. It always seeks to eat away at your confidence, defeat your courage and spirit, while at the same time blocking your access, denying you opportunities, and withholding essential resources.

As a child, my parents, community, church, and school helped to shield me from some of the harsh realities of the crippling racism we faced. By the grace of God, in spite of the horrible, societal, racial and socio-economic disparities, I was able to take advantage of the "separate and unequal" crumbs that fell to the floor of society and thrive. **"In all these things we are more than conquerors through Him that loved us"** (Romans 6:37).

I was facing insurmountable odds, against a foe with which I was unfamiliar. With the help and support of my family and community, I survived the overt racial discrimination and prejudices of my youth. Now, here I stood, going up against an elusive, covert, and well-armed "great giant", the SBA; the bastion of a more insidious and dangerous form of racism, unlike any I had previously known- institutionalized racial, gender, and age discrimination.

For the most part, the racism I faced in my youth was driven by feelings of superiority by those who held the racist views. Very few of them had much power, other than through intimidation, to act on those feelings in ways that could actually harm me. Now I was entering an arena where those, with whom I had to deal at the SBA and in other institutions, had the authority and power to make fine, critical, and grave distinctions and treatments on factors other than my individual merit. They had the power to discriminate, and they did!

I mentioned earlier that the financing application process for women and minorities was not *user-friendly*, and it truly was not. Based on studies and my experience, minority entrepreneurs are historically treated significantly different from their white counterparts when applying for financing; a situation that still exists today. Women and minority applicants are offered less information about loan opportunities, less resources, and less application help by loan officers. However, they are asked more questions about their personal finances.

When I first encountered the SBA, it was a living case of David vs. Goliath. Their acts were of furious intimidation and fierce discouragements, with an underlying dispiriting effort, aimed to defeat me. Scripture tell us how the sole intent of a certain one, the enemy, **"is to kill, steal and destroy"** (John 10:10). There were, without a doubt, unjust practices and actions designed to crush, strip, and consume the hope of my spirit. They were also in place to undermine my determination, my commitment, my confidence, and to shatter my faith. However, I would not be discouraged or defeated, because early in my life, I had crossed my very own painfully rugged, Sinai Desert. I had already learned how to fight great giants.

Throughout the process, I faced obstacles in completing the loan application. The application process was never explained to me, and my SBA loan officer would not provide me with a complete loan package. Rather, she would only issue me small sections of my application package at a time. I would complete that section of the application and wait for months to find out if it was correct. It was as if I was taking a blind test. I was never given instructions, or a tutorial, to help understand all the application requirements. I therefore, was left feeling frustrated and bewildered. Without providing feedback, she would schedule another appointment for three to four months later.

Typically, the same parts of the application I submitted previously were returned to me, months later, marked *"incomplete"*. With no further comments or directions, another appointment would be scheduled for another three or more months into the future. Throughout those months, I would scour the documents, trying hard to figure out the problems or what was needed. At the end, I would once again return the documents to her. Then, three or more months later, the same documents were usually returned to me marked "incomplete" and without any specific reasons provided. Still, there were no personal feedback, written instructions, clarifications, or assistance of any sort provided to me. At this point, I realized my application could be held up for months, because of minor criteria that had very little to do with my qualifications; such as an initial, a signature, a date, *the crossing of a 't', or dotting of an 'i'*. When I requested help with unclear items, there was no assistance nor any resources provided.

Then, after more than twelve months of repeating this submit, wait, and resubmit process, it was clear I was not getting anywhere. This extremely long and frustrating process was maddening. As hard as I tried, I was still not advised what the issues were. I finally recognized and admitted this process was intentional. It was meant for me to get "no-where". Still, I refused to allow this "booby trap" to diminish my self-esteem and self-worth, or make me feel incompetent and insecure. When I began to feel low in spirit, the Lord reminded me again, that I am more than a conqueror. ***"The one who loves us gives us an overwhelming victory in all these difficulties"*** (Romans 9:37). My loan officer's obvious attempts to sabotage my application continued to repeat itself for almost two years.

I then made up my mind that I would refuse to allow my dreams and visions to become stagnate, derailed or defeated. While it was clear by law, that I had the *right* to receive funding, the status-quo practices were designed not to allow me the opportunity to access that funding. I faced people with the power to make "fine, critical, and grave distinctions" about me that had nothing to do with my personal qualifications. I now realized that I was facing someone who could exercise the power to discriminate in any subtle way they wished. I also noted that I was facing someone who was, at the moment, exercising that power. While I was certain my loan officer would find any reason to reject my documents, I had no other recourse but to continue working with her. I clearly realized, it was

I who needed to come up with a change; a way to counteract the prevailing practices of the status quo.

In my despair, I cried out to the Lord. "WHAT SHOULD I DO?" There in Deuteronomy 20:1 He encourages, *"When you go to war against your enemies and ...an army greater than yours, do not be afraid of them, because the LORD your God, who brought you up out of Egypt, will be with you."* At any time in your trials, have you heard what I heard? Filled with guidance, instruction, courage, and covenants, the very first thing the next morning, I once again returned to my loan officer's office with the loan documents. I was still being continuously rejected, however, I would no longer allow a wasted three or four months to pass. Every day, four to five days a week, I was at the SBA's office. Many times, I was already sitting in the main waiting area before she arrived. All day I waited; before and after her lunch, I still waited all afternoon.

Strong and Courageous in the Lord

While I waited in expectation, hoping to be seen, I did not sit idly. I decided to make lemonade out of my lemons. With my mind and heart on the dream the Lord had given me, each day I'd take out my briefcase, and continue to work at developing various aspects of my business plan. Ironically, their waiting room became my workstation.

Repeatedly, my officer would attempt to rush past, trying to ignore me. Feeling extremely anxious, but with an excited smile on my face, I'd quickly stand-up. Digging deep to use the gifts of the spirit in my voice, I'd politely ask, *"Ms. Jane Doe, may I please have just five, or a few minutes of your time?"* Repeatedly, with a sharp, hasty tone in her voice, she would abruptly tell me, "No"! Or, "I don't have time." Or, "You don't have an appointment." But, each day I would return. Many days I felt depleted. Countless times I was certain I was their only client that entire week; especially since I was the only person waiting all day, from morning until the end of the work day. But, day after day, I was denied. Still, it seemed that nothing was changing. This went on from a three-month period until the next three months. The message was clear; she was only going to see me on my scheduled appointment, three months later.

One of my steadfast scriptures which encourages and pushes me forward is Joshua 1. The Lord God Himself repeatedly spoke to Joshua as he pursued unexplored new visions from God saying, ***"Be strong and very courageous in the Lord and the power of His Might;" "Be very strong and only courageous." "Again I say, only be strong and of great courage."*** God Himself told me to **"Be Encouraged"**. In my adversity, His encouragement kept lifting me up. Continually He encourages, "you can do it". God's plans provided me the abilities, and His power kept me in His promise. I did not know when it would happen, but each day I went believing, and expecting I would get the financial package needed for my business approved.

Finally, my break-through came during another scheduled three-month appointment. Although my loan officer was barely a few years beyond my age and a woman, I was fully aware that she did not respect me as her equal. Nonetheless, at that point, she had primary SBA decision-making power over my future business opportunities. She was hanging on to my application and I needed a quarter of million-dollars in financing.

As I sat there, at that moment, the Holy Spirit assured me, ***"The LORD your God is the one who goes with you to fight for you against your enemies to give you victory"*** (Deuteronomy 20:4).

Right away, He gave me the courage to speak up. As I gathered my composure, I gracefully leaned forward. With a polite smile on my face, I looked directly at her and made eye contact. Settling myself, as I took a long, slow, deep-breath, I calmly confronted her. With candor in my voice, respectfully I asked, *"Miss. Jane Doe, how long are we going to continue like this? I am very sure by now you know I am not going away. But, I do need you to communicate with me. I need you to guide me in this application process. I also need you to inform me of the SBA's requirements, because I am committed to securing this loan."*

With forthrightness, I had spoken to her woman-to-woman. My voice was heard. In that moment, I realized I had made it clear; I deserved access to required resources, and expected the opportunity to get it. Even greater, I had required her to see me for who I am. There was indeed a shifting in the atmosphere.

My Defining Moment

It reminded me of an incident from youth. One hot summer day, while preparing to cook a yummy peach cobbler, my mother hurriedly sent my older brother to the store to get a bag of sugar. My brother, youngest sister, and I hopped in the car. We rushed into the grocery store just as we had many times before. Eagerly, my sister and I ran to the soft drink machine in the back corner of the store to get our favorite ice cold bottles of soda; a cold, chilled, bright Red Strawberry Crush for her and a frosty Orange Sun Crush for me.

My brother stood at the front counter talking with the boy behind the counter. They were both about the same age. Even though at that time, racial segregation was the way of the south, it was not unusual after school and during the summer, for the black boys and white boys to regularly play together.

At that moment, I clearly heard my brother say, *"Hey, man I just saw you yesterday, what is wrong with you?"* My sister and I were concentrating on our icy cold sodas, when suddenly my brother throws the bag of sugar on the countertop; just as we were about to take a nice refreshing, cold sip. He grabbed the soft drinks out of our hands, while pushing us out the door. Angrily he yelled to the boy, *"Call... you... Mr.? I -will- never - call -you –Mr.!"*

I heard in my brother's voice a sense of betrayal, humiliation, rage, anger, deceit, and insult. My brother had just been told that, although all the boys were about to turn sixteen years old, the white boy's father had told him that he had to make the black boys call him "Mr." My brother not only refused to call the boy Mr., he also refused to complete our purchases, and went elsewhere to buy the sugar. At that defining moment, the reality of the boys' relationship was flagrantly revealed, defined, and then swiftly ended.

Even though I had a lot at stake, I, like my brother, had stood-up for myself. God saves us and vindicates us from our enemies— whoever or whatever they maybe. **"O God, my vindicator!" My righteous God! When I was in distress, you set me free..."** (Psalms 4:1).

I learned that all forms of discrimination are lethal weapons; they are trials from the enemy, but God uses them as life lessons, as He did in the case of Joseph and his brothers in Genesis (50:20). Joseph graciously explains, **"But as for you, you thought evil against me; but God meant it unto good, to bring to pass, as it is this day."** My loan officer had bad intentions for me, but God turned them into a good outcome.

Over three years later, through God's grace, I secured approximately a quarter million-dollar financial package from a combination of the SBA and banks. Nationwide, this financial package was considered un-pioneered, unprecedented, and unchartered territory, especially in my particular region. "It had happened!" The iron gates were broken; they were pried open! I had become the first African American woman to secure a major SBA and bank financial package in the State of Wisconsin.

CHAPTER 5

A Need for Encouragement

* * *

In addition to the difficulties I encountered working with the SBA, I was also impacted by a lack of supportive services for minority and women owned businesses. At that time, there were no minority small business associations, women small business associations, small business resource centers, incubators, or any other start-up support, advisory or advocacy services to provide guidance.

Equally as disheartening for me, I had no one to encourage me. Early on, I realized others were not always there for me to depend on for help, encouragement, or to understand my dreams and visions. This lack of support even included some friends, family, and members of my community. There was no one in the natural to walk with, motivate, guide, energize, and mentor me; not even to help push me up my steep, narrow, and winding hill. However, words of discouragements were all around. I was constantly told, *"You can't do that,";* *"They are not going to give you that loan,"* or *"No one 'Black' has ever done that."* Their doubts were real to them. Crippling experiences from their encounters with the giant-wizard, had shrouded their confidence. After all, fear and doubt were the historical legacies of dealing with SBA and other financial institutions. Even in the absence of others, the Lord had continued to be there, reassuring me to **"Be Encouraged"**.

Once again, while going through a valley, my greatest encouragement and comfort came from the Holy Spirit. His powerful plan does not always work like a simple flow chart. In my case, it also did not come quickly. God's ways are not based on our plans or thoughts. He knew all the hurdles I would face, as was stated in Jeremiah 1:5. My loving Father affirmed, ***"He knew me before I was in my mother's womb."*** When He formed me, in my mother's womb, He placed purpose in me. He called me to an unchangeable truth; He requires us to only have faith and obey.

On my journey to realizing my dream I had faced many challenges, obstacles, and road blocks. I needed to **"Be Encouraged"**. It is His desire that we, ***"Encourage one another, and build each other up"*** (I Thessalonians 5:11). When there was no one else, my source was in His Word; inspiring me on. Not only did I get God's wisdom, but I also got His grace.

Along the way, m*y life lessons learned were:*

- *That faith and acting in obedience to God, is what releases the wisdom and power of His grace to work in my life.*

- *Faith only focuses on hope, and presses past issues and road-blocks.*

- *Faith does not figure things out in our natural senses.*

- *To attentively listen to God, because, "What God has for you is for you."*

- *From my many life challenges to believe I had "it", before the "it's" of my life were manifested.*
- *To guard and protect my dreams.*
- *To "guide" my faith to trust in God.*
- *My less than enough were precious nuggets, that had developed into infallible, priceless treasures along the way.*
- *To use my faith currency.*

I was certain that God's plan for me was to help bring light to the world. It was confirmed through His word (Matthew 5:14). I was beaming, my heart was filled with joy and excitement. Through my discovery, developing, and use of the gifts He had given me, God opened doors that I could not have opened myself.

Becoming an Encourager

God, who has provided everything for my salvation through Jesus Christ, would through Him, also provide all that I needed to live for His glory. ***"My God will meet all your needs, according to the riches of his glory, in Christ Jesus"*** (Philippians 6:19). He has given us all, the same unique boundless gifts of the spirit: love, joy, peace, patience, kindness, goodness, and faithfulness (Galatians 5:22-23); while providing uniquely different *means* of utilizing our talents. God's spiritual gifts are not to be hoarded, but are 'acts of favor' God has given each of us to share with others. 1 Corinthians 12:7 teaches us the purpose of our spiritual gift, ***"A spiritual gift is given to each of us so we help others."*** He had shown me that, contrary to the ways of society, His gifts of grace should be generously used to help others; not taking a critical *"foot on the neck"*, or *"pull yourself up by your own boot straps"* approach, which we often take.

I realized my life's purpose: To inspire, enrich, and encourage others to discover, know and love their amazing gifts that He has given; while empowering all to also "be their best 'self', even with real imperfections". The business He had provided me, Edel's Day Spa, was my perfect platform from which to fulfill my purpose.

From the beginning, it was evident that God was moving to meet my needs. Just before opening my business, we started to stage my marketing campaign. I soon realized that because of the unique niche of my business, the media and other marketing channels were readily available. I had a constant presence with the area's wide newspapers, radio, and TV stations.

My clientele was primarily well-established professionals and/or up and coming professional women and men who were seeking higher career opportunities. Their goals included career advancement, entry into entrepreneurship, civic leadership, as well as other professional endeavors. They quickly began to look to Edel's Day Spa to provide the professional image and confidence-building consultations they needed, to gain a competitive advantage.

The vision God had given me was etched in my heart. I'd been captivated by the compelling and revealing conviction between the single-minded indwelling Holy Spirit, and the seamless purpose of "looking good and feeling good"; both spiritually and physically. I had been pierced by the challenge and I understood His important command. He requires each of us to give the utmost physical and spiritual, health and wellness care to His temple in every way; body, spirit, and soul. By the time I opened my business, I understood how to walk in my purpose. I was astonished at the level of joy our services brought to my clients and to me. We were equally, very pleased with the outstanding results they received from Edel's spa treatments and services. It was a very organic relationship. Their spiritual and physical renewal was transformative. Clients would come in one way; often tired, burned-out, empty, and insecure in their sense of self image and career presence; but would leave refreshed, rejuvenated, and rewarded with a feeling of well-being. God's empowering *(anointing)* was upon me, and like Moses, I carefully sought out and built a staff with the same fruits that God had instilled in me.

God had provided me a platform to truly be a temple-keeper; to enrich, inspire, encourage, and empower others to excel in their personal and business lives. In addition to being His servant, I was a professional, spiritual, and physical caretaker of God's temples. While doing His will, God made available to me the desires of my heart. Now he was laying out His order; His way of doing things, for me.

I was well prepared both in the natural and in the spiritual convictions He had given to operate this business. It was most gratifying. Edel's Day Spa operated with one standard, EXCELLENCE; and in accordance to the "Godly temple-keeper principles" of:

- Integrity.

- Loving others as Christ loves me.

- Treating others as I wish to be treated.

- Maintaining self-control; by not returning insult for insult in retaliation.

- Speaking respectfully and kindly, one to another.
- Giving a helping hand to others.
- Teaching with understanding.
- Leading by faith and with honor.
- Bringing, without fail, encouragement to His temples.

In order to become the temple-keeper, I knew God wanted me to be, I had to dig deeper within myself and become even closer to the Lord. I was a businesswoman, a leader, an encourager, and a confidence builder; not only to my staff, but also to my hundreds of clients and patrons. They looked to me for coaching; to enable them to successfully meet their everyday professional, social, and personal challenges. In that same manner, through my church, the Lord called me to disciple, fellowship, and to become sister and friend to hundreds of more women for over twenty-two years. I used my business and church platforms to provide encouragement, particularly, to those who were pursuing dreams and visions much bigger than what they could achieve on their own.

Along our way, simple, priceless words and acts of encouragements to friends, family, colleagues, associates, strangers, and as well as to yourself, can be a life supporting transfusion. Most importantly, it is God's plan.

CHAPTER 6

Becoming Spirit Builders

* * *

The life of an entrepreneur or a small business owner is unique. It can be many things. It can be up and sometimes, unexpectedly, it will be down. It can be very exciting, rewarding, joyful, prosperous, and definitely many times, it feels very stressful and alone.

Powerful and encouraging words of truth from God are like cream in your coffee and light in your dark moments. An encouragement goes straight to the heart and connects to God's truth. **"Be Encouraged"** words function as "spirit builders" filled with Power!!! They can add pep to your step. Its energy is like the beam of a fog light to a distressed ship on the raging roaring sea; it will help you navigate safely to reach your destination. ***"For the Spirit God gave us does not make us timid, but gives us power, love and self-discipline"*** (II Timothy 1:7).

It is your God given heritage to use "spirit builders". They are compassionate words from your heart, filled with infused power. They have the resourceful abilities to *transform, ignite, energize, inspire, uplift, motivate, spur-on, stir-up, revitalize, fortify, empower, and invigorate yourself and others.*

Our words of encouragement can rejuvenate a downtrodden spirit and infuse it with confidence. Encouragement gives life, whereas, negativity defeats and kills the spirit. On the other hand, a defeated spirit will devour your dreams. **"Let no corrupting talk come out of your mouths, but only such as is good for building up, as fits the occasion, that it may give grace to those who hear"** (Ephesians 4:29).

Encouragement charges your mood, revs up your engine, and tops off your gas tank. In this small way, it gives the powerful extra boost needed to overcome a challenging experience. Your encouragements can re-energize a weak and broken spirit. They can inspire you and others with the courage to persevere and to follow your life's dreams. **"Be Encouraged"!!!** Everybody needs it. Again I say, **"Be Encouraged"**. In our world, words of despair are all around; from the highest places, even within the pinnacle of the church. God has promised, **"It is He (His words) that overcomes it all"** (John 16:33).

CHAPTER 7

Six Godly Principles for Success in Business and Life

*　*　*

I. PUT GOD FIRST

Putting God first never starts with our head. Putting God first starts in our heart. God promised, when you put Him first, *"You can accomplish everything you need"* (Proverbs 4:22). Putting God First sounds like an option. In truth, it is not. I accepted this truth early in my life because I believed it is possible *"To gain all the world, but lose your soul"* (Mark 8:35, Matthew 16:26).

Drifting Away

There were times when I felt being a businesswoman, spouse, and committed parent with PTA conferences, soccer matches, basketball games, and other commitments did not leave me time to do anything else; most crucial, including spending my quality time with God. These things were so important to me that they caused me to slowly drift and be pulled away from God. I found myself becoming unfocused and off point. Drifting, being pulled away slowly, from our position in Him, is a costly and dangerous place to find oneself. So many times, we are not even aware of the costly threats to our personal and spiritual well-being.

I often, jokingly, would say, I was born on the front pew of the church. I thought I already had a solid foundation in God; but what I was missing, was to make more time for God in my life. I have long known that God desires to be first, in everything pertaining to my life. Putting God first allows Him to uphold this affirmation; ***"I can do all things though Christ who strength me"*** (Philippians 4:13). I needed to seek Him first in every miniscule way, as well as the very big things in my life. He fortifies and assures, ***"The Lord will give grace and glory; no good thing will He withhold from those who walk uprightly"*** (Psalms 84:11). The bible promises, ***"Those who discover these words live, really live; body and soul..."*** (Proverbs 4:22; Matthew 16:26).

The Joy of Reconnecting

When I shifted my priorities back, once again I put God first. I gave Him the fragments of my life that had begun to crumble. Then, I learned to honestly spend time in His presence. Through prayer, I began to talk with the Lord. I learned to 'open up', and give Him complete access by being transparent. Then, I learned to sit quietly in His presence and attentively focus to hear Him. As I studied His word, I enjoyed His presence; I gave him more and more of my attention. He gave me substance to meditate upon, all throughout my day.

I learned to release my spirit, listen to God speak, and allow Him to move through me; even as I drove quietly in my car, during my lunch or shopping about, and especially while I cared for my clients.

My long, warm, and early morning showers became a refreshing sanctuary, as well as a healing altar before the Lord. Sitting silently in His peaceful presence, I could just let Him have His way. He filled me up with the peace, joy, assurance, and abundant wisdom that could only come from Him. His word clearly states, it's as a ***"Peace that the world cannot give you"*** (John 14:28). He gives an assured outcome, ***"If you remain in me and my words remain in you, you may ask for anything you want, and it will be granted!"*** (John 15:7). I found myself wanting to be, continuously, in "oneness" with Him. His door was always open to me, it was boundless. He had given me, ***"A peace which transcends every understanding"*** (Philippians 4:7).

Truthfully, spending time with God, is much like having a heart-to-heart conversation with my very best friend; only better. I thirst to hear everything. Eagerly, I cling to every word said. It is so exciting to connect, and it's almost impossible to put my conversation on hold until the next time we talk. My transparency with Him was through His word. Studying while allowing Him to speak to me in His word, is what created a transformation in me.

Every day of our lives, our physical bodies form and collect old, dry, dead waste materials that must be cleaned off. When our body is not washed clean, health and hygiene problems develop. If left unattended for too long, other more serious conditions will occur. We set aside time to cleanse our physical body from head-to-toes with delightful refreshing emollients, and nourish it with enjoyable natural foods until filled. Likewise, time with God results in setting aside spiritual time to refresh, wash, clean, and feed our spirit. Just as it is necessary to eat and bathe each day; it is also essential to do so spiritually. 'Spiritual dryness' comes when we smother out His time; substituting other things for the restoration that only God can give, through daily time with Him.

I learned a long time ago, that all those things which were so important to me, were also important to God. He reminded me that, either way, they first belonged to Him. He wanted me to bring everything to Him. He wanted me to set aside time with Him; to bring all that was important to both of us (God and me), to Him.

II. WRITE YOUR VISION DOWN

Proverbs 29:18 counsels us, *"Where there is no vision, the people perish: but he that keepeth the law, happy is he."*

As He speaks and gives visions, He also encourages us to **WRITE THE VISION**. As God explains the powerful purpose of His amazing revelation to you, it is to be written down; to help create a clear and comprehensive "picture" of your business and life goals, for a definite, expected time in the future. Your vision will describe what to expect on this date; God's unseen promise. It may very well be something that has never been done, as of yet. It will birth life, by the degree of your faith and obedience. It is the substance of what *you* are hoping for. When our faith and hope work together, it will create a photographic road map of your vision. Your vision will provide a vivid picture of the who, what, when, where, and how. It is an architectural design, a brilliant blueprint to your future! God told Habakkuk, that a vision is a plan, which must *"provide directions at its appointed time"*.

God established the standards for business success, in the same manner, as He did for life. Habakkuk 2:2-3 plainly tells us, *"**The Lord said**, Put the vision in writing and make it clear..., so that you may go quickly."* He explains, *"For the vision is yet for an appointed*

time; but at the end it will speak, and it will not lie, because it will surely come." Did you get it? Here are God's keys to achieving your goals. Were they clear to you? First, let's be sure we understand what a vision is, where it comes from, why it is so important to capture it, why it must be clear, and what it must achieve.

A vision is a clear and accurate understanding of a divine purpose revealed through a revelation from God; to bring about His Will. Let's recognize who said it. God said it. He called Habakkuk to write the vision, "to hear His voice", and cautioned him to make it clear. Like Jacob, sometimes we have a problem embracing God's word, and we too wrestle with knowing His voice. It is important to recognize God's voice. He reveals His vision to those that are able to acknowledge His voice. This can only take place through our spirit. All too often, when we hear the voice of God, we discount it as, "something told me" and disregard it by saying "I'll do it later".

Seven Characteristics

God's instructions provided seven essential characteristics to a godly vision. Seven is the number of divine completeness and perfection (Genesis 1).

God tells us to:

1. "Write it"; *capture it.*
2. "Make it plain"; *get clarity.*
3. "Go quickly"; *provides direction.*
4. "For an appointed time"; *it is a process.*
5. "It will speak"; *He provides a plan.*
6. "It will not lie"; *it is His word.*

7. "It will surely come"; *His promise.*

Capturing your vision is crucial to realizing your dream. For this reason, you may wish to keep a notebook/pad and pen; or, your favorite electronic recording device, such as cellphone, iPad, or computer, etc., with you always.

Did you ever have a dream? A wonderful dream? The vision was very clear in your dream, but no matter how hard you tried the next morning, you could not remember it. It is important to understand, that *capturing* God's vision often comes in the form of a test and with a sacrifice. These "inspired" moments rarely occur when you may feel it is your most convenient time. The scripture tells us, that God gives these visions when we are in deep sleep. ***"He speaks in dreams, in visions of the night, when deep sleep falls on people as they lie in their beds"*** (Job 33:15). Please read it again. What amazing wisdom!

- Who speaks? *God speaks.*

- How does God speak? *He speaks in dreams, night visions.*

- When does He speak? *When deep sleep falls.*

- Where does He speak? *As you lie in your bed.*

As you can tell, there is something of a test and a price involved. To receive clear, blessed directions from God, are you willing to give up, at the moment, what feels good to you? Will you do what you need in, order to get what you want? Are you willing to exchange your deep, restful, relaxing, peaceful, and feel-good sleep for what God has in store for you, in His timing and in His way? If not, this is where you can miss out. God's goodness is not for the faint of heart. Your stumble may very well begin here.

I mentioned earlier that God's instructions provide seven essential aspects to a godly vision. God Himself maps out for us through His GPS, "God's Positioning System", how to hear, acknowledge, understand, and accept His vision. However, all too often, when we awaken from the dream, we are only able to acknowledge, for sure, that we had one. We are certain that the dream was important and we grow anxious and frustrated because try as we may, we are unable to recall it. Sometimes, God will give us this type of dream, over and over again. Then, after a while, the dream disappears. Because of a lack of priorities, it may never return. In the book of Ezekiel, God asked Ezekiel, "Can these dry dead bones live again?" In that valley place, lies many bodies of dry dead bones with unfulfilled destinies. Why? Because of disobedience to God's plan.

I had learned that keeping a "business plan" notebook or a Word document with me at all times, was extremely beneficial. To capture the vision God is giving you, it is essential that you immediately write the vision down. Record His words exactly as He has given them to you. Do not second guess them. I encourage you to make *this* your priority. Without a doubt, if you wait until later to try to write the vision down, you will miss God's manifested message to you. At that point, you will most likely write your own interpretation. Obedient submission to God is principle. The consequence of disobedience is completely missing the vision and blessing God has for you.

Listen, While Writing

When we receive great and mighty treasures from God, He requires an exchange: *All of you, your ways, your timing, and your will; for all of Him, His ways, His timing, and His will.* Whether we are physically or spiritually asleep, the scripture teaches us an all important lesson; at the moment God speaks to us, we must wake up, get up, and get out of our comfort zone. Take your pen and paper, then quietly move with urgency, into the presence of God, and in that moment, quickly write down only what is given to your spirit.

DO NOT become distracted. This is not the time to try to process it, to try to figure it out, or to become anxious about it. After you have written it down and given God praise and thanksgiving, it is now time to ask Him for wisdom and understanding. Proverbs 2:5 says, **"For the LORD gives wisdom; from His mouth come knowledge and understanding."** For this reason, His word tells us to, **"Seek ye first the kingdom of God and His righteousness and all these things shall be added unto you"** (Matthew 6:33). God wants us to seek and depend on Him to open pathways for us.

No one knows the mind of God (Roman 11:34). Only He can make clear His understanding. Matthews (5:6) states, **"God blesses those who hunger and thirst for righteousness, for they will be satisfied."** *Rise up* when God speaks; you will be richly rewarded. Like a clear, fresh fountain of living water, ideas, thoughts, and concepts will flow with complete clarity. Again, do not try to process it, or think it through, or over-think it. Just continue to write.

Have you already had such an experience? If so, the Lord has poured out refreshing streams of directions upon the plans He has for you. Spiritually and physically surrender yourself. As you write, let only the Lord take over and speak to you. Do not worry, or concern yourself about correct spelling, grammar, content, and the like; only ensure that you are attentive in your spiritual hearing. The flesh *(mind)* will try to interrupt. Press-in, listen while you write down what the Lord is placing in your spirit. I have found, the longer you stay in His presence, the longer His stream flows. If you have already had this encounter, were you filled with complete surrender? With peace? With joy and confidence? Were you, like me, bursting with absolute assurance and courageous zeal? This is the Lord, encouraging you; assuring you, to **"Be Encouraged"**. He is with you. Then for certain, you know, if God is in it, He will complete that which He began.

Spiritual Affirmations

Just as important as writing down your vision for your business, your spiritual vision goes hand-in-hand with it. A **spiritual affirmations vision board** is an essential guide for identifying those areas where you need to improve in your spiritual journey. My spiritual affirmations were crucial to successfully building my business. My spiritual affirmations were filled with rich biblical and godly encouragements. They kept me grounded and affirmed to me; *who I am, whose I am, and what I am capable of accomplishing.* My spiritual affirmations vision board constantly assured me of God's promises. My business vision and spiritual affirmation board were the wind beneath my feet; pushing me forward toward my goal, by encouraging me. It helped affirm my connectedness with the Lord, while showing, sustaining, strengthening, and encouraging me in those areas where I needed godly fortification. It will help give you clarity as to whom you need to walk along next to, and the type of spiritual resources you need.

"Without a vision, the people perish..." (Proverbs 29:18). God's promised and purposed outcome for writing down His given vision is, *"Because it (the vision) will surely come."* The word of God clearly provides the vision He has given. One of my vision board affirmations is Proverbs 7:3; He calls us to be totally committed to Him, to, *"Write them (His Word) on the tablets of your heart, and, to wear them <u>like</u> a ring on your finger."*

III. DREAM BIG

It has been said, "Reach for the moon, and if you fall, you can at least grab a hand full of stars on the way down!"

Society has saturated us with these kinds of sayings. So many of them limit the potential of our dreams, water-down our visions, and make powerless our goals. We are inundated with hopeless expectations through quotations that sound like words of wisdom. But many are just elixirs that lure us into accepting limitations of mediocrity. We often use worldly words thought to be encouraging or have wisdom, while in fact, they are opposite of our Lord's word. In today's culture, all too often, we look-up to and hold in high esteem the words of people based on their wealth, social, celebrity, or public status. The word of God says, *"Place your faith and confidence in Him who is able to keep you from falling"* (Jude 1:24). *"The LORD will be your confidence and will keep your foot from being caught"* (Proverbs 3:26).

Adhere to His word and expect His favor. There comes a time when we must put "our" period and exclamation marks on our faith. God's out-pouring of favor is based on our ability to believe that His plan is to prosper us and to keep us from falling (Jude 1:24).

You can do nothing without a dream. Dream His dream; a dream so big only God can fulfill it. A big dream is not based on the physical size of your business or life goals, but, on the magnitude of your unlimited, passionate ability to pursue it by faith.

Does your dream draw you forth? From the beginning, He placed a *desire and dream* in my heart. When your dream is from God, you are drawn to it by Him. Then, you can plug-into the celestial galaxy of God's amazing grace.

Assess the Source

First test your dream to assess: *"Is the dream too big for me to fulfill without God's help?"* When you think about it, does it overwhelm you with excitement? Most importantly, do you have the slightest idea how you are going to make it happen? When my dream was first revealed to me, I was overwhelmed. I had written down the dreams, vision, goals, and plans; however, God's vision for me was too big for me to handle by myself. I did not have the slightest idea where to start. In the natural, I could not figure it out. But, true to His word, God provided me with His road map. John 16:12 instructs, **"Do what you can do and what you know to be correct, right now. Then He will show you what to do next."**

If your answer is yes, you can do it without His help, then you are not dreaming dreams from God. On the other hand, if it's much bigger than you are, **"Be Encouraged."** Stay focused. Stick-with-it! You are indeed on-the-right-track!

God's dreams contain goals established with visions so powerful that they ignite your heart, and flood your deepest inner spirit with overwhelming joy at the very thought of them. Any dream God puts in your heart will be much, much bigger than you are. May I encourage you to not attempt to move too fast?

Don't Be Too Eager

Be mindful, the flesh, or "self-will", will become eager; raging like your prized stallion at the Kentucky Derby, anxious to break loose. Charging out the gate of *unpreparedness*, rushing and straining to run at the fastest possible pace on its own, it can and will be spooked by the least thing. James 1:7-8 speaks with candor, ***"That person should not expect to receive anything from the Lord. Such a person is double-minded and unstable in all they do."*** Don't try to get in front of God! Consider, you are at a meeting and you state an awesome idea. Then, immediately, someone else restates your excellent idea as though it was their own, attempting to take complete ownership. Is this you? Those with small visions and pride will become anxious and will often try to restate and re-define God's plans. Trying to move or run too fast on your own is not God's will. In the long run, we cannot succeed at anything more nor less than what "that still, small quiet voice" inside of us speaks and directs. It will only come to pass within the time He has planned, if we have the patience, courage, and faith to remain in His plan. This is why His Word says, ***"Glory belongs to God, whose power is at work in us".*** Our God assures, ***"By this power He can do infinitely more than we can ask or imagine"*** (Ephesians 3:20). Here the book of Ephesians clearly gives us the definition of success. It is God's power at work in us, to do infinitely more than we can ask or imagine. Wow! My amazing, awesome God!

The Lord Will Make a Way

As I pursued my dreams, I needed to know my strengths and weaknesses, and so will you. This was truly the time when I needed to seek God's faithful resources. I asked Him to give me a heart open to accepting His truth, for honest transparency within myself. God took away *so much* pressure. He helped me to become transparent before Him. I allowed Him to remove and take away my weighted bonds of insecurity, pride, worry, guilty, fear, doubt, and so much more. I became stronger in His power. He restored me with a clean spirit, through a true knowledge and acceptance of self. He empowered me in my weakness, and showed me how to utilize my strengths, which he is still doing today. Everything you will ever need, He has already provided for you (I Peter 1:3). I had to willingly accept and trust in His way.

In addition to capturing your vision and dream, this is the time to fully hear from God. Then, you must become prepared and equipped. You will need to do things such as research and learn everything about your new business interest, its governances, market niche, your competition, and your local, state and industry requirements. You may also need to get certified in required areas, attend workshops, take classes, start saving money, stabilize and/or clean-up your credit history, and work on your business plan. Begin to network; connecting with the person(s) He has set aside for you, by developing relationships with your bankers, joining professional groups, volunteering, engaging with and supporting someone else's vision, and much more. Unquestionably, a deep, trusting relationship with the Lord is key. Make sure you are honoring God with your spirit and time, by keeping a true and authentic relationship with Him. In His time, God will help you achieve your goals.

In today's commercialized society there is an excess of self-centered, do-it-yourself *feel-good mantras*. Self-help classes, books, magazines, slogans, articles, blogs, social/commercial media, and the like, all emphasize some form of new contemporary trends and man-made quick-fixes. I encourage you to accept only the authentic, steadfast truth. I John 4:1 encourages, ***"Beloved, do not believe every spirit, but test the spirits to see whether they are from God, for many false prophets have gone out into the world."*** A sound and consistent bible study, bible-based book club, fellowship, or study group along with a daily surrendered prayer-time will help you develop your foundation and sustain you on your journey.

Remember, dreams from God will draw, prepare, and keep you balanced; if you stay in His will. God has a way of placing people and resources in your life just for you. You may think you are inadequate, not important enough, or too small or unknown; not a member of the "in-crowd", not as attractive, not as educated, or not a member of the same ethnic group or gender as others in your chosen field. My fellow "child of God," again, **"Be Encouraged"**. Just-show-up. Continue going forward. Continue to prepare! Take each "next step", one step at a time. Trust God as your strength and your source, although His timing is not your timing, and His ways are not your ways (Isaiah 55:8). Each day move forward, listening to and expecting ***"Your (God's) will to be done"*** (Matthew 6:10). Once more, **"Be Encouraged"**. God meets you at the level of your expectations. Believe! "Truly believe" and have a clear vision in your mind as you move forward daily to fulfill the big, and what may feel impossible, dream that He has placed in you. Build your plans according only to the God given vision you have written down. **Now, trust God to show you the way** (Psalms 37:5).

IV. GO FOR THE GOAL

Your goal refers to or describes your purpose. What's your goal? What have you done toward achieving it? Your great dream will not get you anywhere if you don't go for it. When God gives dreams and visions, He also has an assurance destiny. Focus on the vision and goal God has inspired in you. Your visions will provide the road map, with directions, that help guide you towards understanding and achieving your desired future. Your goal inspires and encourages you to turn your vision into your God given reality.

God Given Goals

I learned that a God given goal is complete. It does not create imbalances in our lives. It will seamlessly create a cohesive balance between our family, spiritual, business, financial, social, emotional/mental, and health/wellness responsibilities. Without goals, we can become distracted and drift aimlessly, devoid of getting where we need to go.

Scripture tells us; ***"My goal is that they may be encouraged ... I want them to have complete confidence that they understand God's mysterious plan..."*** (Colossians 2:2). A godly inspired goal will encourage us to have complete confidence in God's plans. It will *seem to come "naturally"*. It produces a burning inspired excitement inside. Often times, even from childhood, we recognize this burning hope.

Consider, that the little child who sings and dances so beautifully, or the ones that are curious, imaginative, and creative; also the ones who are so loving and nurturing have all been given their inspiration and drive by God. As a young child, God spoke vision into Jeremiah.

He affirmed, ***"I know the plans I have for you, declares the Lord, plans to prosper you and not to harm you, plans to give you hope and a future"*** (Jeremiah 29:11 NIV). Who made this declaration? It was the Lord God Himself. God's plans *never* fail. I learned God has already created a *seven-fold security plan* to safeguard His purpose in us. He spoke His seven-fold security plan to me, and assured:

- *I know.* God Himself knows the plans He has.
- *I have.* He has plans just for me you.
- *The Lord declares.* He affirmed His plans.
- *I have plans to prosper you.* He prospered all of my needs; physically, spiritually, and emotionally.
- *I have plans not to harm.* He has plans of safety for you. He kept me safe, protected, and healed me.
- *I have plans to give you hope.* He gave me a deep faith foundation when I could not see what I was hoping for.
- *I have plans to give you a future.* He gave (and gives) me an assured future.

I learned that to fulfill this God given goal, there are times you must get "alone" with the Lord. Alone, in a secret place, just for you and Him. Yes, a physical place is needed, away from all the noise. Especially important now, I had also learned that to keep a spiritual place with unconditional entrance to the Lord, is what safeguards and protects our access to Him.

In this spiritual place, I saw God's plans through eight (8) essential, perfectly formed, and sequential standards. When we seek God with all our heart, to show us our purpose, then He will answer. When we place *nothing* ahead of the Lord, He takes us to a whole new level of awareness. He lets us know a new beginning and a new day has come: **"Then, (1) you will call on me (2) and come (3) and pray to me, and**

(4) I will listen to you. (5) You will seek me and (6) find me (7) when you seek me (8) with all your heart" (Jeremiah 29:12).

He promised new doors will open, and you will find Him, if you are persistent with all your heart. He opened doors to my dreams and visions, which were so much bigger than me, which I could not open on my own.

God's plans are what is best for us. However, there were times when I did not understand why things were happening in my business or my personal life. There were times when it *seemed* God had withheld His promise from me. As a believer, while in flight to my dream, times came when God turned up the heat to "refine" me.

Tested by Fire

We are God's golden nuggets. Yet, to be refined and achieve pure gold in us, we must feel the fire of trials and testing. It will serve to sift our impurities; those situations which can hold us back from achieving our dreams. God, and God alone has to remove these obstacles from our lives. Through this refining God sheds light on the obstacles of our lives. Once we accept His guiding light and acknowledge that the true power to make better decisions is ours; then, and only then, do we shift in the right direction toward our dreams and visions.

This process is walked out a bit differently in each of our lives. For me, important relationships fell apart. There were times when others betrayed, deceived, falsely accused, misled, and misjudged me. There were also moments when I met financial challenges and money was not there to meet my personal or business needs. I faced sicknesses and other hardships. Additionally, I found myself still struggling with issues that I thought I had long ago conquered. He knows His time and thoughts for me. Therefore, I recognize, that He is still refining me. God is always seeking to teach, perfect, and protect us. Only then can our golden nuggets be turned into pure gold by the refiner.

Don't Give Up

Going for the goal requires a refining and purifying process. It can involve an especially confusing encounter to those of us who have been seeking the Lord, and for those who are drawn to a deeper, more intimate relationship with Him than ever before. Although we may not understand why it seems God is *allowing* "bad" things to happen in our lives, His word tells us; **"He knows the way that I take; when He has tested me, I will come forth as pure gold"** (Job 23:10). Yet, **"All things work together for those who are called by His name and for His purpose"** (Roman 8:28).

Reaching your goal may take what seems like a slow pace, mine certainly did. May I encourage you to continue to follow through by your faith? Hear the Lord, listen to Him, and obey. He is purifying you as gold; preparing you to go for the goal. He promised, **"This is the victory that has overcome the world—our faith"** (I John 5:4).

V. GO THROUGH THE VALLEY

When God gave freedom and great abundance to the Israelites, it still took them forty long years before they reached the great destiny God had for them. They started their journey to victory with unspeakable joy and excitement. But on their way, *God's children* gave up, and settled in the valley of the desert's wilderness. More disturbingly, fear and uncertainty caused them to want to return to their place of despair and bondage. They were more than half-way to their destiny, just a few days away from their new promotion in life. A life filled with the exceeding goodness and blessings God had already prepared awaited them.

Keep the Faith

So why did they want to turn back? What happened? The same thing that can happen to anyone, and often does, in business, career, or life. It was because they lost their faith and determination (Judges 2:13-14). They took their eyes off the vision, the same as we sometimes do. Their faith muscles became weak, out of shape and weary, from time in their Sinai Dessert. Without their familiar, everyday food; Mickie D's, Popeye's, or KFC fast food restaurants, or their comfortable Holiday Inn or Motel Six, they were out of their old, familiar routine and environment. Traveling to their new destiny was discouragingly long and hard; very cold at night, then extreme heat and humidity by day. Their wilderness trip grew to feel desolate and dreadfully unforgiving. On their journey, their faith and dependence on God strayed and became dangerously weakened. They forgot the vision God had given to them. In the wilderness valley, the promises of God grew dim in their minds.

Wilderness valleys are those places and times, of going through circumstances, where things go wrong. Just as life does not always work out the way you'd hoped, neither will your business. A dark time may come and you are unable to understand why. There, in those valley places, is the time to build up your faith muscles. In the valley, on the back side of the mountain, is where Moses learned the great leadership skills necessary to handle the business of God. He learned to humble himself through the lessons of endurance from his father-in-law Jethro (Exodus 18:24). A wilderness place is where he encountered God's true plan for his life. Our loving Father was creating in him a humble heart that was dependent upon God.

God's Personal Development Program

On the backside of my mountain, in my valley place, I like Moses, experienced God's personal development plan for me. Once again, early one Christmas morning, my life was changed. While I was making a quick run to the grocery store, a distracted driver sped into the front driver's side of my car. Pieces of my car were scattered all over the street. Astonishingly, the accident took place directly in front of my church. I heard my soul crying out; repeatedly praising God with thanksgiving, saying, "Thank you for saving me Father!", "Thank you for saving me Father!" While I was lying there in severe pain on that freezing cold Christmas morning, I had a spiritual encounter with the Lord.

Suddenly, I was reminded by the Lord that on two different occasions, by the same pastor, it had been prophesied to me that *God was calling me in a new direction.* In my own nature, I was overjoyed. I had received the prophesies as a confirmation of my plans, because at the times of the prophesies, I was right in the middle of building greater opportunities for success with a major new business expansion plan. God had shown my business His favor and I had clients from all over the country. While lying there, in that cold street, God revealed to me that my business plan was not the plans He had for me at that time. We must be careful, for this was a clear situation of me not hearing in the spirit, but only in the natural. When I reflected, it reminded me of the young priest in I Kings 13. He truly loved God and he had been called to be a temple-keeper, however, on his mission he became distracted and deceived.

As an aesthetician, my hands were essential to my business. On that day, my body was badly injured. My arms, hands, and fingers had sustained severe damage, and I could hardly move. While in my valley moments, I recalled that I was given His prophetic message, which I did not understand at the time; God's plan was to take my spiritual relationship with Him to a higher place. However, I had failed to recognize that I had not unconditionally yielded to Him. During my lengthy recovery, the very same pastor prophesied the very same message to me a third time. It then became clear to me, that God was taking me in a new direction.

In my infirmities, the Lord was causing me to know Him even more as my *solvent* God. By His amazing grace, the Lord had saved my life. As with Moses, it was on the backside of my mountain, in my valley place, where I learned so much more about myself and the higher purpose of submitting to Him.

The Lord showed me that (Exodus 3):

- I had not truthfully listened to His message to me.
- I had not spiritually heard His call.
- I had not adhered to His message.
- I had not yielded my plans to His plans.

Not listening denies our ability to hear God, to obey Him, and to allow Him to direct our path. With deep humility I immediately repented before the Lord.

With all of God's children, as it was with me, the valley place is God's spiritual physical therapy clinic. A place set aside where He builds-up, perfects, and strengthens us to carry out His purposed plans for our lives. Jeremiah called his encounter, "the potter's wheel" experience (Jeremiah 18). In order for God to use Jeremiah as He had planned, Jeremiah, just as I, required some spiritual physical therapy.

God may not send or speak a prophetic word through someone else to us on a regular basis, but He is always with us. Jesus said, *"Surely I am with you always, to the very end of the age"* (Matthew 28:20). There will be a time when God will call you to another place in Him. What I had to learn, was to listen with my spirit, not just my natural self, to God's calling. He said, *"My thoughts are nothing like your thoughts, says the LORD. And my ways are far beyond anything you could imagine"* (Isaiah 55:9). You too, may well be in God's personal development program. **"Be Encouraged!"**

In your valley experience, spend time revisiting God's vision for you. Seek and listen to God. Make sure your path is the one God chose for you, now. Then, give it your full zeal! Know this; surely as you pursue God's plans, *"stuff will happen"*. What is my point? Sooner or later, unexpected distractions will come knocking, be they personal, financial, relational, emotional, health, family, or spiritual. But, stay the course.

Write your vision as He gives it to you. Regularly review your written vision plan. Spend time listening to God. Go back and re-examine your vision plan; most importantly, seek a deeper understanding from God. Ensure you are not working on plan A with plan B's strategy. Romans 15:4 tells us, *"Whatever was written in former days was written for our instruction, that through endurance and through the encouragement of the Scriptures we might have hope."* Why must we remain vigilant?

God's word teaches us it is for:
1. Instruction
2. Endurance
3. Encouragement
4. Hope.

What does it produce? *Hope*.

The Power of Hope

Our hope is the engine that drives *our* faith, which produces our determination to get through the valley. When we lose strength in our hope muscle, we are guaranteed to lose direction. A lack of direction leads to the likelihood of unfilled dreams, incomplete plans, missed opportunities, and unrealized destinies. It will bring about death to your dreams (James 1:15). From the beginning, He gave us a choice; to choose Him and His way or choose our own way.

Many amazing plans that God has already provided for His children have gone unexplored and unfulfilled. Why? Because we gave-up. The journey grew too long, the required commitment seemed too hard, the resources were too little, and we lost our determination. In II Chronicles 15:7, the word of God encourages, *"But as for you, be strong and do not give up, for your work will be rewarded."*

Press-in, *set-up a specific, well planned faith exercise program.* Faith is our life-giving substance of what we do not yet see. It is the driving force that pushes and pulls us to our victory. Hebrews 11:1 explains it clearly, *"Faith is the substance of things hoped for, the evidence of things not seen."*

God encourages us, "Do not get stuck in the valley". Psalms 23 acknowledges it as a place where we are to go-through. Keep moving forward and fear not! He knows the attacks that will be launched against us to bring about self-doubt, causing us to question our faith, willpower, abilities, and courage. All of the attacks are attempts to pickpocket God's plan by keeping us stuck. Remember, God tells us in John 10:10, **"The thief comes only to *steal and *kill and *destroy; I have come so that they may have life, and may have it more abundantly."** What an amazing, eye-opening promise from God. *On my journey, I had to hold-fast to this wisdom and assurance from my Father, to sustain me whenever I felt self-doubt.* Peter, the one on whose faith Christ Jesus chose to build the church, said, **"Dear friends, don't be surprised at the fiery trials you are going through..."** (1 Peter 4:12). He too was very familiar with just how the plans God has for our lives are under attack.

A valley can be the enemy of our faith. Therefore, I learned it was important for me to identify and to become fully knowledgeable of what it was that had tried to ensnare my faith; that is, *what were my test?* I had to get to know them by name, to determine their level of present and future impact on me, as well as those around me. I also had to determine the damaging effect they had already created. Then, I had to fight with all of my God given power, to pass those tests in order to achieve my goals. Daily I denounced, and with God's help overcame the things that were trying to ensnare me including illness, racism, self-doubt, and others. I realized that all these things were simply distraction and I knew that I must stay focused on God's plan for me.

Overcoming Distractions

In scripture after scripture, the Lord continues to encourage, do not get distracted in your valley; *"Wait on the Lord without distractions"* (I Corinthians 7:35). It was, and still is, essential to start my day with prayer, praises, and thanksgiving for everything; both large and small that He has done in my life, and to affirm His love, grace, care, and plans for me. Constantly encouraging *yourself* in His word is a requirement for overcoming any distractions placed in your *valley*.

When problems occur, the *Distraction Family* will send out members of its "Welcome wagon club." This gang of distractors sets up snares to pull you off course. They take residence in the valley of your spirit, intending to trap and defeat. We all know the under-handed members of this family; they will even invite you to their party. Their headline marquee reads, "For members only." The starring attractions include *deception, distress, distortion, denial, doubt, defensiveness, depressions, and all their "Distraction" relatives.* They cling to your heart, feed by your fear. Then, they dance circles around you and manipulate your mind, whisper lies into the ear of your spirit, take your thoughts captive, and like locusts, obliterate your confidence as they trample upon your dream.

When life's issues happen to cause you to get off course, or to fall, do not allow yourself to become isolated and all alone. Most importantly, seek encouraging and righteous counsel from the word of God, through a person with a strong, mature and godly foundation. God's plans and purposes for you have not changed. If He planned your dreams and visions, He will get you through the valley. He knows our journey, but *we choose our paths.*

Be Aware of Pride

Sometimes the path we choose leads us away from God's path and causes us to fall. Such was the case of King Nebuchadnezzar, ruler over all the people, nations, and languages of all the earth. He was profiled and ranked as the number one top rated, most powerful and wealthiest ruler in the whole-wide world. His wealth was inconceivable, he flourished in all his lavish palaces and he was at the height of great success.

In our success, we must stay intensely watchful, for the sin of becoming puffed-up by the contaminating poisons of *self-pride, arrogance, and self-conceit*. These pathological viruses will infect and ruin great success. They are like heat seeking missiles that zero in on the mind and spirit, while steadily trying to take all of God's glory for themselves. The book of Daniel, Chapter 4 gives a full account of the prevailing truth of King Nebuchadnezzar.

The Lord knows how to bring temperance to those attacked by these degenerate traits: ***"Pride goes before destruction, and a haughty spirit before a fall"*** (Proverbs 16:18). ***"I will crush the arrogance of the proud and the haughtiness of the mighty"*** (Isaiah 13:11).

Imbued with power and wealth; this mighty, royal, well cultured, sophisticated, yet decadent and despicable King lost his mind. He fell miserably from his extravagant royalty into hopeless despair; living among animals of the wild.

Pride, arrogance, and self-conceit are depravities that often plague great or powerful individuals. God promised that such will plunge you into ***"a place of weeds and salt pits… a wasteland…."*** (Zephaniah 2:9). However, the opposite of self-aggrandizing pride, is humility. Philippians 2:3 offers the purist delineation: ***"Do nothing out of selfish ambition or vain conceit, but in humility consider others better than yourselves"***.

God Gives Grace to the Humble

God restored and gave grace to the king, once he humbled himself to The Most-High KING. He confessed, *"After this time had passed, I, Nebuchadnezzar, looked up to heaven. My sanity returned, and I praised and worshiped the Most-High and honored the one who lives forever"* (Daniel 4:34).

With the same tender compassion, God will give grace and consolation, when we humble ourselves and call upon His guidance. *"Clothe yourselves with humility toward one another, because God opposes the proud but gives grace to the humble"* (1 Peter 5:5).

At some point in your life, you will find yourself in a battle ensnared by distractors. Just as pathological viruses such as pride, arrogance, and self-conceit can get you into your valley; a humble gracious spirit can form the foundation which allows God to get you to where you need to go.

Create a strong legacy for yourself, go forth, grounded by a spirit filled with *delightfulness, determination, direction, and discipline. Get Back Up!* **"Be Encouraged"**.

VI. BE AN ENCOURAGER!

"Dearly Beloved, I pray that in all respects you may prosper and be in good health, just as your soul prospers" (3 John 1:2). You are so special to God. You were born to be victorious. It brings Him joy when His children are living out His first command; to *"be fruitful and multiply"* (Genesis 1:28). Achieving our dreams is connected, together, with our ability to believe, receive, and walk out His words of encouragement. He is our master counselor and chief encourager. He assures us of His plan for our lives. It is *"to prosper, and be in*

good health, as our soul prospers in Him " (3 John 1:2). As we receive God's encouragements, His loving compassion draws us to Him. When we allow God to draw us, He transforms our relationship with Him. God becomes our comforter. He infuses us with the endurance to withstand difficult and challenging circumstances by continuously inspiring us to **"Be Encouraged"**.

The word *"encourage"* appears over 100 times in the Bible's New Testament alone. My God inspired book provides immeasurable and unwavering *pearls of wisdom,* along with God's rich, nourishing **"Be Encouraged"**-food, for success.

I have selected and included in my book powerful words of affirmation that have inspired, sustained, and empowered me spiritually in my pursuit of my dreams and visions. I encourage you to select, read, and post these encouraging Spiritual Affirmations as you go forth in pursuit of "your" life's dreams and visions. Allow them to continuously transform and become your standards for everyday living.

Plant them as seeds of encouragements in your spirit. Place them in key areas throughout your home, workspace, business, or phone; where you can constantly see them. Read and think on them daily and continuously. Meditate on them in your heart. Regularly, throughout your day, speak these promised affirmations of God out loud into your spirit. Yes, speak them out loud, then take time to let them penetrate, deep inside. Proverbs 3:3 encourages, ***"...Wear them like a necklace; write them on the tablets of your heart...", "And in the morning, rising up a great while before day, Jesus went out, and departed into a solitary place, and there prayed"*** (Mark 1:35). Follow in the footsteps of Jesus Christ. Like Him, I found out that when starting out my morning with "set aside" time with God, He was and is my power, my peace, my patience, and my enduring source. I have learned that, whatever situation we are facing, it is vitally important to use the word of God that applies to that specific situation.

A regular diet of God's truth is essential to maintaining sustainability in our journey through life and in your business. It is not the amount of time that we spend with God, it is the quality of the time we spend with Him, that pleases Him.

He has destined something inside of you; as you continue fulfilling your- yet to- be discovered gifts, dreams, and purposes, ***"I am confident of this very (one) thing, that He who began a good work in you will perfect it until the day of Christ Jesus"*** (Philippians 1:6).

"Lastly, receive your power from the Lord and from His mighty strength" (Ephesians 6:10).

"BE ENCOURAGED"!

This book is now yours, please read it as often as you may need; to **"Be Encouraged"!**

BE ENCOURAGED – *As You Follow Your Dreams & Visions*

My Reflections to You

This precious, God inspired book contains six **"BE ENCOURAGED" Principles**; with proven biblical practices to help you wherever you are in the pursuit of your dreams and visions; for business, career, relationships and life. Standing on His covenant promises, I was determined to seek, ask, and listen to God's plans which were filled with essential keys to victories for my life.

You too, are just who God wants. He blesses our brokenness, strengthens our faith, and guides us into our purpose by assuring, *"I will give you beauty for your ashes"* (Isaiah 61:3); when you, *"Seek first his kingdom and his righteousness, and all these things will be given to you as well"* (Matthew 6:33). **"Be Encouraged"**.

Now, thirty-five years after I started on my journey, I am thankful to be able to share with you some well-seasoned, unfailing, and powerful life nuggets. My life experiences have molded in me a temple-caretaker relationship. Like the relationship between a football quarterback and receiver, this relationship produced a deeper and deeper dependence on the Holy Spirit inside of me. He has given indisputable treasures for each of us to overcome roadblocks and to pursue our dreams. My trials were a vast, and many times, rugged terrain. There were no quick, one answer instant fixes.

When you go through your valleys and shadows, it won't always be easy. **"Be Encouraged."** Get plugged-in, continue to press-in to the life source from which all prevailing powers flows. Nothing is more POWERFUL! *"Now these things happened to them as an example, but they were written down for our instruction…"* (I Corinthians 10:11). Along my journey, God's promises, standards, commands, directions, and grace that He formed in my spirit's faith, became the lamps unto my feet. It is with joy that I give God all praise and glory, by sharing them with you on your journey; that you too may **BE ENCOURAGED! LIVE ENCOURAGED! STAY ENCOURAGED!**

*"And this is the confidence
that we have in Him,
that, If we ask any thing according to His will,
He Heareth us,
And if we know that He hears us.
Whatever we ask.
We know that we have the petitions that
We desired of Him"*

(I John 5:14-15).

BE ENCOURAGED – *As You Follow Your Dreams & Visions*

Spiritual Affirmations for Your Dreams & Visions

BE ENCOURAGED as you pursue dreams and visions from God. Each day recite out loud these words of godly affirmations. These Spiritual Affirmations will purify your spirit, anchor the dynamic of your faith, and affirm who and what you trust in; that you truly may know that nothing is impossible with God.

* * *

Write Them on the Tablets of Your Heart

Spiritual Affirmations

I am the child of God. (Galatians 3:26)

I am counting my BLESSINGS today! (Colossians 4:2)

I am whole and complete. (Mark 5:34).

I am thankful You keep me in good health. (3John 2:3)

I am divinely set apart to be a world-changer. (John 15:8)

I am blessed with godly dreams and visions. (Zerchariah 2)

I am guided and protected by God. (Psalms 121:7)

I am the head and not the tail. (Deuteronomy 28:13)

I am righteously appointed by God to do great and mighty works. (John 15:16)

I am thankful You have made me to prosper. (3John 1:2)

I am able to do all things through Christ who strengthens me. (3 John 2)

I am able to exceedingly abundantly above and beyond all I can ask or imagine. (Ephesian 3:20)

I am thankful that no good thing will You withhold from me. (Psalms 84:11)

I am grateful that my works are pleasing to You. (Romans 12:2)

I am blessed to be a blessing… In the name of Jesus. (Gensis 12:2)

Thank you Father. Amen. I will
Be Encouraged! Live Encouraged! Stay Encouraged!

Daily Prayers & Confessions

Father God, today I thank you. I affirm that it is You who provides all the resources to all my needs, to develop and grow my business as I increase abundantly in my life-
I will rejoice in the Lord always. I know the Lord is near me.
The God of peace is with me.
I receive the peace of God, which transcends
all understanding,
I will let my gentleness be evident to all.
I will not be anxious about anything, but in every situation, by prayer and petition, with thanksgiving, I will present my requests to God.
I will guard my heart and my minds in
Christ Jesus.
I will think only on whatever is true, noble, right, pure, lovely, admirable—excellent or praiseworthy.
I can do all things through him who
gives me strength.
My God will meet all my needs according to the riches of His glory in Christ Jesus (Philippians 4).

Thank you Father. I will
Be Encouraged! Live Encouraged! Stay Encouraged!
Amen.

My Prayer for You

Father, as this, your child, steps out in faith in the name of Jesus. I pray, that you will walk in God's Grace, per His promises. I give praise and thanksgiving for the fullest of His manifestations to you in your life. *"Now unto His who is able to keep you from falling and present you faultless before the presence of His glory with exceedingly joy..."* (Jude 1:24).
In Jesus, Amen.

Thank you Father. Amen.
Be Encouraged! Live Encouraged! Stay Encouraged!

Self-Reflections

I have provided a list of Self-Reflections on lessons learned derived from each chapter. They are to aid you in your own intimate, transparent time with God. Worksheets are provided to help inspire spiritual and personal transformation. The worksheets may be used in several ways; in formal and informal groups, small study groups, or during personal intimate time alone with God.

*** *Please be willing to be transparent.*

CHAPTER 1
UNIQUELY CALLED
"RECOGNIZING YOUR PURPOSE"

Self-Reflections

Below are Self-Reflections on lessons learned. As you seek your **Unique Calling**; they are to aid you as you enter an intimate, transparent time with God. This worksheet may be used in formal or informal small study groups, or during personal intimate reflection time with God.

LESSONS I LEARNED

☐ Do you believe you have a unique calling on your life?
☐ Have you acknowledged (acted on) the unique calling on your life? If yes, what do you believe you are called or appointed to do?
☐ Are you walking in your unique calling? State why or why not.

Answer/Discuss:

_____

_____

_____

_____

_____

_____

* * *

SELF-REFLECTIONS

☐ If you have experienced distractions or attacks against your dream, identify the attacks against you based on the word of God. Call it out. Be very specific. (Mark 11:23).
Answer/Discuss:

___

___

___

___

___

___

* * *

☐ Do you have an encouragement scripture/s that you stand on?
☐ How often do you claim its power and authority?
Answer/Discuss:

___

___

___

___

___

___

☐ What is your GPS (God's Positioning System)?
Answer/Discuss:

_____

_____

_____

_____

_____

_____

* * *

☐ Like your system in your car, how often do you spend time using your GPS?
Answer/Discuss:

_____

_____

_____

_____

_____

_____

_____

CHAPTER 2
YEA THOUGH I WALKED THROUGH THE VALLEY AND SHADOWS...

Psalms 23:4

Self-Reflections

Below are Self-Reflections on lessons learned. They are to aid you in your own intimate, transparent time with God as you reflect on **Your Walk Through Your Valley and Shadow** (Psalms 23:4). This worksheet maybe used in many ways. It may be used in formal and informal groups, small study groups, or during personal intimate time alone with God.

LESSONS I LEARNED

☐ *I learned that trials are special preparedness-tests which God will use to launch you into your future.* ☐ What are/were your preparedness test? (Romans 4:17). ☐ How is God preparing you? (Psalms 23:4).

Reflections/Discussion:

_____

_____

_____

_____

_____

☐ From the very beginning I learned about trusting God. (Jeremiah 1:5).
Reflections/Discussion:

___

* * *

☐ *I learned the spiritual principle of,* ***"Call that which is not as though it already is"*** (Romans 4:17).
Reflections/Discussion:

CHAPTER 3
ALL THINGS ARE POSSIBLE TO HIM WHO BELIEVES...

> Matthew 9:22

Self-Reflections

Below are Self-Reflections on lessons learned. They are to aid you in your own intimate, transparent time with God as you reflect on **All Things Are Possible to Him Who Believes** (Matthews 9:22). This worksheet maybe used in several ways. It may be used in formal and informal groups, small study groups, or during personal intimate time alone with God.

LESSONS I LEARNED

☐ *I learned the lesson and deep understanding of true faith* (Hebrews 11:1).

Reflections/Discussion:

_____

_____

_____

_____

_____

_____

_____

☐ *I learned, how you see yourself is your bridge that connects you to your ability to dream* (II Corinthians 5:19).
Reflections/Discussion:

_____

_____

_____

_____

_____

_____

* * *

☐ *I learned how visions and dreams meet opportunity.*
Reflections/Discussion:

_____

_____

_____

_____

_____

_____

SELF-REFLECTIONS

☐ *How has the Lord reminded you of who He is in your life?*
Reflections/Discussion:

_____

_____

_____

_____

_____

_____

_____

_____

_____

_____

_____

_____

_____

_____

CHAPTER 4
GOD TURNS OPPORTUNITY INTO REALITY

Self-Reflections

Below are Self-Reflections on lessons learned. They are to aid you in your own intimate, transparent time with God as **God Turns Opportunity into Reality.** This worksheet maybe used in many ways. It may be used in formal and informal groups, small study groups, or during personal intimate time alone with God.

LESSONS I LEARNED
☐ *I learned to live my profound belief...* (Matthew 5:14)
Reflections/Discussion:

_____

_____

_____

_____

_____

_____

_____

☐ *God had taught me the enduring determination and bravery of a warrior. To "be strong", to be "an over-comer"* (Joshua 1:6, 7, 8, 9).
Reflections/Discussion:

_____

_____

_____

_____

_____

* * *

☐ *Have you ever had a David and Goliath situation?* ☐ *What was your dotting the "i" and crossing the "t" crossroad in your life?*
Reflections/Discussion:

_____

_____

_____

_____

_____

_____

☐ *I learned how to and, whom to seek for directions.*
Reflections/Discussion:

_____
_____
_____
_____
_____
_____

* * *

☐ *I learned* that trials are the enemy's lethal weapons, but, they are God's teaching tools.
Reflections/Discussion:

_____
_____
_____
_____
_____
_____
_____
_____

CHAPTER 5
A NEED FOR ENCOURAGEMENT

Self-Reflections

Below are Self-Reflections on lessons learned. They are to aid you in your own intimate, transparent time with God as you reflect on **A Need for Encouragement.** This worksheet maybe used in several ways. It may be used in formal and informal groups, small study groups, or during personal intimate time alone with God.

LESSONS I LEARNED

☐ *I learned to use my faith currency* (Mark 11:24, John 11:40).
Reflections/Discussion:

_____

_____

_____

_____

_____

_____

_____

☐ *I learned the purpose of spiritual gifts.* ☐ *What is a spiritual gift?* ☐ *What is/are your spiritual gift/s?* ☐ *How does God want all of us to use our spiritual gift?* ☐ *How is your spiritual gift used to carryout God's will in the world?*

_____

_____

_____

_____

_____

* * *

☐ *I learned to* **"Seek first the kingdom of God and His righteousness"** and to trust His promise, that, **"Then, all these things taken together will be given unto you (me)"** (Matthew 6:33). **Reflections/Discussion:**

_____

_____

_____

_____

_____

☐ *I learned faith in God is what releases the wisdom and power of His grace to work in my life.* ☐ Is this your life's biggest lesson? If not, what was it, and how did affect you?
Reflections/Discussion:

___

___

___

___

___

* * *

☐ God's promised standards, acts, directions and grace that He formed in my spiritual faith became the lamp unto my feet along my journeys. ☐ Is this true for you? Please be clear about your journey
Reflections/Discussion:

___

___

___

___

___

___

Chapter 6
BECOMING SPIRIT-BUILDERS

Self-Reflections
Below are Self-Reflections on lessons learned. As you seek to **Become Spirit-Builders**, they are to aid you as you enter an intimate, transparent time with God. This worksheet may be used in formal or informal small study groups, or, during personal intimate reflection time with God.

LESSONS I LEARNED
☐ Are you a spirit-builder? If yes, how are you a "spirit-builder"? If no, why not?
Reflections/Discussion:

_____

_____

_____

_____

_____

_____

_____

_____

SELF-REFLECTIONS

☐ How are you using your words?
Reflections/Discussion:

_____

_____

_____

_____

_____

* * *

☐ What are the three words you use most to describe or refer to yourself?
Reflections/Discussion:

_____

_____

_____

_____

_____

_____

☐ What are the three words you use most to describe or refer to your family, i.e.: siblings, children or spouse?
Reflections/Discussion:

_____

_____

_____

_____

_____

* * *

☐ What are the three words you use most to describe or refer to others outside of your home, i.e.: friends and colleagues, etc.?
Reflections/Discussion:

_____

_____

_____

_____

_____

_____

SELF-REFLECTIONS

☐ How do others perceive your words? ☐ How do they hear and receive them?

Reflections/Discussion:

___

* * *

☐ Do your word build up or do they tear down?

Reflections/Discussion:

- ☐ What are your key words of encouragement?

Reflections/Discussion:

* * *

- ☐ How often do you use your words of encouragement?

Reflections/Discussion:

☐ Are your words different for family; friends; colleagues; or yourself? How are they different? ☐ Why are they different? ☐ This is an important question to reflect on, and to lay before the Lord.
Reflections/Discussion:

_____

_____

_____

_____

* * *

☐ Name at least two other people to whom you can offer encouragement? Can you name more? ☐ Call their names out before the Lord or write down their names.
Reflections/Discussion:

_____

_____

_____

_____

_____

_____

My Pearls of Wisdom

Write Them on the Tablets of Your Heart

Have you ever had a dream so big that all those around told you that it was out of reach? Has self-doubt left you so paralyzed with the fear of failure that you dare not pursue that business venture, job, talent or person of your dream?

*Believe that you have "it" before the "it" of your dream manifests itself in your life...**Be Encouraged!***

*The less than enough in your life now are precious nuggets that can be developed into infallible priceless treasures along your life's journey...**Be Encouraged!***

*An unwavering faith and acting in obedience to God is what will release the wisdom and power of His grace to work in your life...**Be Encouraged!***

*When your financial resources are lacking, God will honor your faith currency...**Be Encouraged!***

"Faith is the confidence that what we hope for will actually happen; it gives us assurance about things we cannot see" (Hebrews 11:1).

Be Encouraged! Live Encouraged! Stay Encouraged!

About the Author

Edna Wayne Mathews is first and foremost a believer in God, in every aspect of her life. She says, "My passion is to help spread the Good News of Jesus Christ by inspiring others all over the world to **"Be Encouraged", and become encouragers to others while they pursue their big dreams.** She is the founder of Encouraging Life Enterprises which is dedicated to empowering others to use their passion to live their purpose and achieve personal and professional dreams and visions that are much bigger than "them".

Edna has been featured in popular industry magazines, as well as nationally known publications such as Jet and Ebony Magazines. She has been profiled in Black Enterprise Magazine, as its "Outstanding Entrepreneur", and in Milwaukee Magazine's "People of the Year" edition. She has shared the story of her business success through appearances on CBS, NBC, and ABC television networks. Edna has been a consultant to local, national magazines, newspapers, and other media outlets.

Be Encouraged! Live Encouraged! Stay Encouraged!

BE ENCOURAGED – *As You Follow Your Dreams & Visions*

© **Copyright 2017 Edna Wayne Mathews**

All rights reserved solely by the author. This book is protected under the copyright laws of the United Stated of America. No portion of this book may be reproduced in any form without the written permission of the author. All rights reserved. No part of this publication may be reproduced, stored in a retrieval system, or transmitted in any form or by any means, electronic, mechanical, photocopying, recording, or otherwise, without the prior written permission of the author.

Unless otherwise indicated, Scripture quotations are taken from the Holy Bible, New International Version®. Copyright © 1973, 1978, 1984 by International Bible Society. Used by permission of Zondervan. All rights reserved.

Scripture quotations marked NLT are from the Holy Bible, New Living Translation, copyright 1996, 2004. Used by permission of Tyndale House Publishers, Inc., Wheaton, Illinois 60189. All rights reserved.

Scripture quotations marked NASB are from the New American Standard Bible®, Copyright © 1960, 1962, 1963, 1968, 1971, 1972, 1973, 1975, 1977, 1995 by The Lockman Foundation. Used by permission. (www.Lockman.org)

Scripture quotations marked AMP are from the Amplified® Bible. Copyright © 1954, 1958, 1962, 1964, 1965, 1987 by The Lockman Foundation. Used by permission. Scripture quotations marked KJV are taken from the King James Version.

Scripture quotations marked MSG are from the Originally published by NavPress in English as THE MESSAGE: The Bible in Contemporary Language copyright 2002 by Eugene Peterson. All rights reserved. (The Message Bible Online).
Edna Wayne Mathews

www.ingramcontent.com/pod-product-compliance
Lightning Source LLC
LaVergne TN
LVHW051134080426
835510LV00018B/2399